The Most Dangerous Gang In America: The NYPD

By

Richard Jeanty

RJ Publications, LLC

Newark, New Jersey

To Therez
Enjoy!

RJ Publications
rjeantay@yahoo.com
www.rjpublications.com

ISBN 0-9769277-9-9

Printed in Canada

May 2007

1 2 3 4 5 6 7 8 9 10

Contents

Acknowledgement

I would like to thank all the usual suspects who have supported me through my writing career and other endeavors. You know who you are.

To my baby girl, Rishanna, I will always love you unconditionally. Thanks for coming into my life. My family will always be first. Thanks to Stacey Murphy for being there.

Thanks to my dad for always for showing a lot of enthusiasm about my work. Special thanks go out to all the book clubs and readers who continue to inspire me to get better with each book. I would like to give a big shout- out to the street vendors and booksellers around the country and all over the world for keeping the world in tune with our literature. Thanks to all the book retailers and distributors who make it possible for our books to reach the people.

A special shout-out goes to all the New York book vendors and entrepreneurs.

A big shout-out goes out to my nephews and nieces as well as my brothers and sisters.

Last but not least, I would like to thank my fellow writers for making reading fun again for our people.

Special thanks to my editor, Nancy Rousseau, for prioritizing this project. I wish I could have given you more time.

INTRODUCTION

Is this book written to add to the controversy that surrounds the NYPD and their senseless killings of innocent Black men? Yes and no. Without a doubt there bounds to be much controversy when a person's life is taken senselessly by anybody. However, my goal for this book is to caution change in police procedures and to remind them of the victims whose lives they have taken unjustifiably and prematurely.

This book is written because not too long from now most people will forget about Amadou Diallo, Sean Bell, Patrick Dorismond and many other victims who died at the hands of the NYPD for no reason other than the fear that a few cowardice cops carried in their hearts.

This book is necessary because I'm a black man living in America and every time I reach for my cell phone on my waist, I could potentially draw fifty shots from a cop who feels as though his life is threatened by my mere presence.

I want to point out that I'm not necessarily offering a lot of new information in this book. Most of the data compiled for this book is easily accessible online through a Google search. Most of the book is commentary coming from me as a black man and as a mouthpiece for those people who might share my views. I didn't have to do too much research to find out the great lengths that police departments around the country go through to establish the modern day lynching of black men. A simple search under "Black Men Killed by Police Officers in America" using any search engine, will bring up hundreds of pages of victims. Most of the killings were unjustified.

Never mind the fact that Black men have to deal with the highest unemployment rate in New York City, the highest school drop out rate, the highest rate of incarceration, but now the violence has become increasingly deadly whenever we have to deal with the police. It's about time someone takes a stand for change. We can't rely on Reverend Al Sharpton and Jesse Jackson to carry the load on their own. Their schedule is too busy fighting injustice across the country. We need to stand up as individuals to demand change in our justice system in all the police departments around the country.

I understand that throughout the book that I might go off on tangents at times and that's because this subject evokes the kind of emotions that are uncontrollable, sometimes. This project was a personal project and the views are personal as well. I'm not an expert in this, but I'm frustrated by it. This book reflects my personal frustrations as well as my anger and determination to demand change. And since no one thought it important enough to talk about, I figured why not me. Getting angry at home and doing nothing about it wasn't going to solve anything. At least with this, I might get some type of dialogue started and maybe even set the motion for some action towards a resolution.

I understand the great risk that I'm taking and the threat to my family by writing this book and taking on the police department. I can confidently say that there's no fear on my part doing that. The greatest fear for me was to stay silent and allow the police to pose an even greater threat to my life every single day.

This book is an eye-opener only for those who care about humanity.

1

What's the Point Of This Book?

I'm actually writing this book to voice my personal frustrations with the police department as well as the justice system. This book is very opinionated and most of the accounts are based on my own personal experiences with the law and police in general. I'm not trying to force my opinions on anybody, just as I would not like the police to infringe on my rights. This book is my own testimony to the world and I want to make sure that people clearly understand my approach in this book. I'm not trying to be tagged a literary genius or anything of that nature. I just wanted to write a book that reflects my struggles and maybe a couple of my friends, family members and a few associates. I know enough people who agree with most of what is written in this book, and I'm sure there will be many more who disagree.

Is there really a need for this book? I would say yes. Most people would be hard pressed to find another major city in any part of the world that typifies multiculturalism or a melting pot, as it is often referred to, more than New York City. There are many people who will probably question the motive behind this book, but I feel it is important to step out of my realm to offer a voice to those who will never be heard. Not only that, I also feel that I owe it to my daughter, future son, grandson and granddaughter as well as myself to let the world hear what's going on with the people who look like me in the City adored by most people in the world. Most people in the world want to visit New York City at least once in their lifetime, so it's only fair that they know about some of the realities of this great city. I had to add my daughter to the equation because a ninety-two-year-old Black woman was shot and killed in an apparent botched raid in Atlanta for suspicion of drugs, but I will expound on that later.

As multicultural as New York City may appear to be, I find that the common factor of police brutality seems to fall mostly on one group and one group only, Black men. Okay, that assessment may not be one hundred percent accurate, our brown comrades, the Latinos, are subjected to the same maltreatment as well. There are many stereotypical reasons why Black men are feared, but I wonder sometimes why the NYPD Officers have so much fear in their hearts for these men. Supposedly, NYPD Officers are called New York's Finest, but why are they involved in so many cowardice acts against unarmed Black and Latino men most of the time?

First of all, I feel that I need to clear up a few things regarding the reasons behind this book. The most important thing to me is the fact that I'm a potential victim. You might be wondering why I feel that I'm a potential victim, but it's plain and simple to the eye, I'm a Black man. I'm feared just because of the melanin in my skin. Have I ever held a gun in my hand? Perhaps I have, just like the many white men in

America who carry guns on their waistbands who go unnoticed everyday, but I'm scrutinized even when it's just a cell phone on my waist. As a matter of fact, my cell-phone is more likely to be a death sentence for me in New York City and I mentioned this in another book that I wrote. I admit to holding a gun at a shooting range on a few occasions in Georgia, but I never carried or intended to carry a concealed weapon to harm anyone. Many police officers, not just the NYPD, have this fear that most Black men walk around with concealed weapons looking to take a shot at them. Sorry, I'm not one of those men and I know many other Black men who don't fit that category. Does that mean that I won't have a police officer, especially in New York City, unload his weapon on me then reload to unload it again? Nope!

Second of all, I must address the fact that this book is not objectively written. I did the best I could and that might be objective enough for some readers. However, if you want real objectivity, I suggest you go find a real journalist out of this country that can objectively portray people who look like me as good people without referring to some stereotypes because those journalists don't exist here. As a black man, I can never be objective in this endeavor. I know far too many people who have been victims of police brutality and abuse. If you're looking for an objective point of view, you bought the wrong book. However, if you're willing to take the time to try to understand the plight of the black man in this country, I might be able to shed some light on that. This book will reflect my own personal experiences professionally, personally and with the law. I'm not abstract to police brutality and abuse because of my ability to put together a few sentences and paragraphs that people can refer to as a book. I'm even hesitant to call this a book because of the backlash I might face for not representing the cops in a good light. But that's no fault of my own. Some of these police officers are doing a great job shining the negative light on themselves. I've even given the opportunity to a few to let their perspectives be heard. It's ultimately up to the reader to decide whether this is pure bullshit or if these things are really going on within the police departments.

I'm not here to represent the cops, but I'll be fair to explain that my book is not a reflection of all cops, just some of them. There are bad apples in every bunch and the police department is no different. The danger, however, lies with the fact that these criminal officers have a gun and badge and they're allowed to shoot at people when they deem necessary. We'll never know that they're criminals or have criminal intent until after the fact and that's what's so scary.

I don't want people to feel that I'm picking on New York City cops, but you have to wonder why the violence against unarmed Black men in New York City is so exponentially greater than anywhere else. It feels kind of odd for me to be using words that are usually not commonly found in my books, but there are those critics who are going to challenge my intelligence. I'm a simple Black man with a college education that I bought from a public university. It wasn't free; I had to pay for it. So, I might as well say I bought it. Does my college degree reduce the risk of me being shot in New York City by a cop? Hell no! It actually increases my chances of being a victim of senseless violence at the hands of cops, because I'm actually one of those determined young man who wanted to succeed at all costs and I happen to enjoy driving a nice car, which places me at a higher risk of being mistaken for a drug dealer. As you read the last line, you're probably wondering if I've indeed sold drugs. I can honestly say that I never have and never will. I have never as much smoked marijuana. I'm not saying that I'm perfect, but I'm not a murderer, drug dealer or any of the other stereotypes attached to black men.

Do I have beef with drug dealers? To a certain extent I do, because they're somewhat responsible for the destruction of our community. I don't condone drugs. Before I even elaborate on this, I want to dispel the myth that most drug dealers are black or Latino. Au contraire, most major drug dealers are white. I could elaborate on the drug thing a little, but I don't want any drug dealers coming after me after reading this book. It's bad enough that the NYPD is going to be hunting me down worse than the most possible violent gang known to man. I don't need to give the NYPD reasons to say that I was shot by drug dealers because of this book. I'm no coward by any means and that's why I undertook this project to let people know what's going on with the most dangerous gang in America, the NYPD. I already know the risks associated with this book and I want to say that fear does not live in me.

Drug dealers are no doubt ignorant bastards, but there's a bigger force behind the creation of these bastards. Drugs are imported into the hood daily and everyday there's a new drug dealer being groomed for the prison system and all that is done by design. The police departments, the prison system, the justice department and only Lord knows how many other departments would be unemployed without the traffic of illegal drugs. The most desperate group to find themselves selling drugs, sometimes even to their mothers, are Black men. Why? You can easily refer to one of my later chapters for your answer. Lack of education feeds the need for ignorance. These people are only selling drugs because of their ignorance. Nobody wants to see their mother, brother, sister, cousin or uncle on drugs, but they're sold on the American dream, whatever that is for some people.

America has set up different dreams for many different people and it's up to the individual to reach for his/her dream. Nobody's born a fool, but many people grow up to become fools because of the set-up and system in America. I can definitely say that I would've never sold drugs even if I absolutely had to in order to survive. Then again, survival is a state of mind. America has taught us that survival is having more than one car and a big house. There are countries where survival is defined as one meal a day for a whole family. I don't know if I was ever sold on the American dream, but not everyone in the hood has the luxury to be as analytical as me. My zeal and desire is stronger than most because I stepped out of the box a long time ago. My destiny has always been decided by me, not by some system. I have faltered along the way in search of my destiny and I almost became a victim of the penal system as it was designed for people like me to a certain extent. I've lost my temper a few times and the cops were more than happy to put me in handcuffs and take me away. I never allowed myself to get out of control where the system would be in control of me as a man, though.

Drugs are an integral part of American life and the US economy. We know about the trillions of dollars the government benefits from the sale and confiscation of drugs every year. Columbia is not an hour drive away from any part of the US, yet cocaine and heroin continue to be the devastating force destroying the Black community. I never came into contact with too many Black pilots with access to planes at their whim, millions of dollars, and security the size of the Chinese army. I know that's what it would take for a Black man to smuggle the amount of drugs that is distributed throughout the Black community on a daily basis. You don't have to travel far to see the devastation of drugs in our community. Newark, New Jersey has been victimized for years. Parts of the Bronx, Queens, Brooklyn, Manhattan and even Long Island have suffered the consequences of drugs as well. The places I named are just a drop in the bucket, but somebody is making money everyday. I'm not talking about the small money that is so prevalent in the hood amongst the drug dealers who think driving a Mercedes Benz signifies that they have arrived. I'm talking about big money, the trillions that the government pockets every year while claiming to be fighting the war on drugs. After all, we're known for starting and fighting wars.

No one has ever called me dumb in my life, but I'm sure that my intelligence has been questioned by many even when my mouth is closed. Well, I have to take back the first statement. The first time I was called dumb was by my high school principal who basically shared the same views as the many prejudice people I've encountered in my life who felt the need to tell me "You're an articulate young man," after hearing me speak. The cops have their own prejudices as well, and I will be talking about that later in this book. Yes, you heard me, a high school principal thought his students were dumb and he still kept his job despite the fact. I'll always remember Mr. Donato's racist views towards the Black students at Hyde Park High School in Boston. His assistant was no better. Ms. Hamilton was just as much a racist, but I heard after I graduated somebody actually complained about her and she was shifted around to a few other high schools in Boston to victimize and characterize other young Black men as stupid and dumb like she did at Hyde Park High. I've gone off course a little, but you will see later how everything that I'm writing is relative to the senseless shooting of these Black men.

The mere fact that the color of my skin is dark and I don't sport a clean cut appearance with an Italian tailor made suit everyday has forced many, including other Black folks, to question not just my intelligence, but also my motive in their presence. It's funny that America was founded by a bunch of societal rejects from England who refused to follow law and order, but yet the media has managed to create an image of Black people in America that is detrimental not just to Black people, but to the nation as a whole.

I know that a lot of this may not be making any sense right now, but I actually plan to go somewhere with it. This is leading to a major point and it's going to be very clear. I never claimed to be a genius. I'm just an average man trying to find solutions to a problem that jeopardizes the daily lives of millions of young men that look like me. So, it's really not that simple. It's very complex. Please bear with me as I collect my thoughts and the proper verbs and nouns to form the correct sentences to relate my message to the masses. I really don't want to be labeled incompetent by some right wing reviewer who's able to convince people that I have no business writing a book. Our president was elected despite the fact that he can't pronounce a word as simple as "nuclear." I, at least, deserve the chance to be heard. Besides, if you've read this far, that means you already bought the book and you might as well finish reading it. If you're going to make any decision or judgment call, you have to be fair and read the whole book. That's all I'm asking for.

You're probably wondering who am I addressing this to, right? Well, at first, I figured this would be a great opportunity to address these young Black men who are considered an endangered species, then I realized that I need the rest of the world to also be part of my audience because this is not a Black or Latino problem, it's a societal problem. Everyone's lives can be affected by the way these young men are viewed. That old white woman who lives in Manhattan, who sometimes has to ride the train after-dark to go fill her prescription for her heart condition is affected. How so, you asked? Apparently, Black men are everywhere, but they seem to be more prevalent in neighborhoods where little white old ladies that carry purses full of cash live. And if that's the case, some poor old white woman would more likely suffer from a heart attack at the sight of a young Black man even if that Black man is coming from a long day's work. Her perception is that he's looking for an easy score and if there's no one in sight to secure her safety from this potential criminal, she might just drop dead on her own. That's dangerous!

I also want a broader audience because this book serves a broader purpose in the fact that many people who live in New York City are totally oblivious to the plight of the Black man. The approach taken in this book was carefully chosen because I had to find my sense of humor in order to write about a subject that is so very serious to the well-being of many inhabitants of the City that are singled out and dealt with in a devastating, murderous and rage-full ways because of their skin color.

Now that I've established some of the reasons behind this project, perhaps I should start going into some of the details. First, I think I need a disclaimer somewhere in this book. I might as well end this chapter with one.

This book is not an open invitation for the NYPD to start harassing me and plant evidence against me to fabricate an illegal case. I also want to say that not all cops are bad cops; we just have more bad cops in New York City. Also, notice to the drug dealers: I'm not dissing you. I just think that you all are a bunch of morons putting my life at risk because we share the same heritage. Stop selling drugs in your community, stop giving these cops reasons to shoot you to death and stop thinking that drug dealing is a profession and a career. The only path this career will lead you is jail or death. With that said, please don't let your ignorance dictate your action.

2

The Victims

Highlighted throughout the next several pages is a sample of victims of police brutality in New York City and the rest of the country. Some of the examples are documented deaths that took place at the hands of New York City police officers according to published reports compiled through my research. The NYPD has killed at least 100 people in the last two and a half years, most of them covered up by official declarations of "justifiable homicide," or however justification could be determined. I can only cover a sample percentage of the murder victims in New York City in the last ten years, for it would take many volumes of my book to feature every single victim.

The common denominator in all of these killings is one thing and one thing only, people of color, more specifically Black and Latino men. Age or gender does not guarantee immunity from the barrel of a New York City police officer's gun, or any cop from any major city around the country for that matter. Grandmothers are killed; sons are killed; mothers are killed; fathers are killed; grandfathers are killed; and even children are killed. When will it stop? Unfortunately, there are more victims being killed around the country everyday as I write this book. Unless accountability is placed on the murdering cops, this will not end anytime soon.

It's sad that the Federal Justice Department is the only place that these murder victims' families can turn to for any type of real justice. The corruption throughout the police departments around the country is rampant and if something is not done soon, we're going to be doomed as a society. Injustice towards one race affects justice towards all races. The ripple affect of injustice will find its way at your front door when you least expect it. It's only so much that people can take.

The victims of police brutality don't necessarily have to be a friend or relative in order for us to be affected as people. If we are to live in a civil society, we must demand that our law enforcement officers act in a civil way and uphold the law that they're sworn to enforce. If every man is supposed to be created equal, how come black men are dying at an unequal and alarming rate at the hands of police?

3

Sean Bell and His Friends

According to published reports in the New York Times, police in Queens, NY, shot and killed a man after his bachelor party. The New York Times reported on Nov. 27, 2006 in the published article titled "50 Shots Fired, And The Experts Offer A Theory." The police account of the events went accordingly: five officers unloaded 50 shots at a bridegroom who, twice rammed his car into a minivan carrying undercover police officers who were investigating club Kalua, while leaving a bachelor party at a strip club. The soon to be married groom, Sean Bell, was killed, and two of his friends were critically wounded, one was hit eleven times.

According to the Times and other news outlets, the shooting on that Saturday unfolded very quickly. None of the victims involved had time to think about making the right decision because the situation was controlled by the police from the very beginning. There was an undercover police officer mingling inside Club Kalua, a site of alleged frequent drug, weapon and prostitution complaints in the Jamaica section of Queens, New York. The officer allegedly overheard a verbal exchange between a stripper and a man that led the officer to suspect the man was armed, Police Commissioner Raymond W. Kelly said later on that Saturday during a press conference. The undercover officer immediately alarmed the officers acting as backup outside, a total number of seven officers, about 4 a.m., setting into motion the events that would take place later that night. A group of men were on their way out the club arguing briefly with another man, when someone from the group said, "Yo, get my gun," Mr. Kelly said. The eight men managed to split into two groups of four, with one group piling into a Nissan Altima driven by Mr. Bell, Commissioner Kelly added. An undercover detective who was following the group on foot approached the vehicle without identifying himself, and Mr. Bell allegedly drove into him, hitting his leg, before plowing into a minivan carrying two backup officers, the commissioner said. The driver backed up, ascending a sidewalk and hitting the front gate of a building before going forward and striking the van again. The officers opened fire, striking Mr. Bell, 23, twice, in the right arm and neck, Commissioner Kelly said. The fatally wounded Bell, died on the way to the hospital, Joseph Guzman, 31, was struck 11 times, and the third man, Trent Benefield, 23, was struck three times. Mr. Kelly said "it was unclear whether there was a fourth man in the car and what became of him."

The details of the event were not concrete. Bob Herbert of the NY Times reported in his column of Nov. 30, 2006 article titled "Badges, Guns And Another Unarmed Victim." The overwhelming efforts of reporters trying to get to the bottom of the story were not as surprised by the cops' actions. The fiancée of Sean Bell visited the narrow street where he took his last breath before he was killed in a barrage of 50 bullets in a rush of judgment by police officers early that Saturday morning, just a few hours before he was to be married. Sean Bell and his two friends were victims of aggressive police behavior. While sitting in their car near club Kalua after attending a bachelor party, a group of undercover cops surge upon Sean Bell and his friends. The case almost appeared to be that the cops wanted something to happen that night as they were on assignment staking out the club. "Here is my first quick take on this case: If I was in my car outside a rowdy nightclub in the wee hours of the morning and someone who looked like a club patron came running toward me, screaming and waving a gun, I would immediately slam the gearshift into drive, hit the accelerator and try to get the hell out of there," said Bob Herbert, the New York Times writer. And it appeared as if Sean Bell and his friends were trying to do just that when they were sprayed with 50 bullets by police.

With the presence of alcohol in their system, the cops were trying their best to blend in with the crowd at the club. Obviously looking for trouble, with evidence of prostitution, underage drinking and illegal guns and more, they went above and beyond the call of duty to discover criminal behavior. They even imagined criminal behavior where none existed. It was said that one of the officers may have believed that one of Sean Bell's friends may have been carrying a gun. No gun was ever found at the scene and there was no evidence that any of the three men were armed at all at any time that night. "It sounds to me like excessive force was used," said Mayor Michael Bloomberg, who described the shooting as "unacceptable" and "inexplicable."

Referring to Mr. Bell and his two friends, the mayor said, "There is no evidence that they were doing anything wrong." "The thing that is most unacceptable about this case is not the total number of shots fired, but the fact that five New York City cops were so willing to begin firing at all -- willing to take the life of another human being, and maybe a number of human beings -- without ever establishing that there was a good reason for doing so" reported Bob Herbert.

The investigation into the shooting is questionable at best. The New York Times reported on Dec. 4, 2006 in their published article, "In Seeking Clues To Police Shooting, A Search And Arrests," that police basically wanted to turn upside down the lives of residents in the area where Sean Bell grew up to help build their case. Detectives investigating the case started rounding up people at a Queens apartment building and seized a semiautomatic weapon and a small amount of marijuana from people unrelated to the shooting, according to their own account. The arrests were supposed to be part of a broad police effort to locate "witnesses" including the infamous made-up "fourth man" in the case, who police believed may have briefly been in Mr. Bell's car on Saturday morning minutes before five police officers fired a barrage of fifty bullets. The arrests only infuriated residents as tensions started to heat up in a sensitive case. One of the people arrested for no reason at all, LaToya Smith, said in an interview that she knew Mr. Benefield only because they lived in the same apartment complex, as well as Mr. Bell, who she said helped her in the past. According to friends and family of the three men, the police were acting overzealously by placing under arrest, those who knew the dead and injured men, and also noted that none of the victims were charged with any crimes. They also questioned the existence of the fourth man. "If he's bionic, and he's that good to get away from those bullets, I want to meet him, too," said Eboni Browning, Mr. Guzman's fiancée, after leaving his bedside at Mary Immaculate Hospital.

According to the New York Times, Police Commissioner Raymond W. Kelly said that the warrant that led to the arrests was executed "in conjunction" with the investigation of the shooting of Mr. Bell. The warrant execution took place as a result of previous purchases of narcotics at that location, where the raid took place," he said at a news conference at One Police Plaza. Outrage and anger filled the hearts of the people at the apartment complex in Queens, where candles and photos were set up in tribute to Mr. Bell. Police have shown disrespect to that community and even in their hour of grief, continued to harass and disrespect those close to the victims. The tone was no different at Mary Immaculate Hospital, where Mr. Benefield and Mr. Guzman were undergoing surgery to save them from their wounds. "I'm enraged," said Bishop Erskine Williams, whose 26-year-old son, Erskine Williams Jr., was arrested on a warrant for an unpaid summons of $25. He was soon released, but not before he was questioned about Sean Bell. "They're harassing a lot of black males where we live, and it's got to stop," the bishop said.

The bishop was part of a group of people who met with Mayor Bloomberg on the Monday following the incident. The police were only interested in questioning his son about Bell's bachelor party because he knows Mr. Guzman and Mr. Benefield. Their intent was to find out whether Benefield, jr. was at the party, and what those involved might have told him. “It's obvious the police need to build a case," said the bishop, who is the pastor of New Seasons Family Worship Center in Jamaica. He said the Smiths are his niece and nephews and that Stanley Smith is the keyboard player at his church.

The bishop went on, “They don't have credible evidence. Their methods are wrong, even if their intentions may be pure.” In a reported interview, his son said that after he spent a night in the hospital watching over Mr. Benefield, detectives checked him for tattoos and pressed him for details about what Mr. Benefield had said. “They know I'm Trent's best friend, “That's why they're harassing me,” said the younger Mr. Erskine. A person by the name of Ducky became a person of interest to the police, as they went about their way terrorizing people at the Baisley Park Gardens complex where the arrests took place. Neighbors said the police were asking about a man nicknamed Ducky. The police commissioner declined to speak about any additional developments in the police investigation. “There was nothing I can do about the skepticism about the existence of a fourth man. The existence of a fourth person is a part of this investigation,” Mr. Kelly said. “It's one of the issues being addressed by investigators.” The police efforts are being led by the same unit of the Internal Affairs Bureau that spearheaded the inquiry into the police shooting of Amadou Diallo, an unarmed African immigrant, seven years ago.

I shouldn't have to explain the intent of the police based on these articles. It's obvious that cover-ups are a part of police business in New York City. If a fourth suspect can miraculously walk away unscathed from a barrage of fifty bullets, what can't the NYPD do within their power? It is business as usual. Kill a black man and make up a reason to justify the killing. Even if more innocent victims have to suffer in order to exonerate the guilty officers. There's an established pattern with the New York City Police Department. No longer are the days of crooked cops carrying rogue guns to set up their victims, now they have new tactics that bring forth new witnesses based on their criminal backgrounds. It's simple and plain, if people don't do what they want, they'll find a reason to make them cooperate, and that's the police way.

As reported by the local newspapers in New York City, in the days following the shooting, even as city officials were assuring community and religious leaders of a fair and thorough investigation, the three men's criminal records, including some sealed juvenile cases, were leaked to the press in what their attorneys said was an effort to "dirty up the victims," This is another common practice by New York City officials that usually follows the deaths of innocent victims at the hands of police. In some unreasonable way, this is supposed to prove that there was reason for the shootings. Police raided apartments in the complex where one of the men lives and another used to hang out. If the men were shot and in the hospital, why is their place of residence being raided? Were the cops trying to coerce someone to come forward to say that these guys had indeed carried guns with them when they went out? And even if they did, they sure as hell weren't carrying them that night. None of it adds up. As many as a dozen friends and acquaintances were taken into custody and questioned. Police officials claimed any arrests in what some describe as a "parallel investigation" were coincidental. It was an attempt at masking the police's disastrous behavior.

"There was about 72 hours where it was just insane. . . . It was cops gone wild," said attorney Charlie King, who represents, at last count, 11 people questioned by police in the aftermath.

Allegations of parallel investigations involving The NYPD are not new. The NYPD have historically made it a priority to conduct parallel investigations while their officers are involved in shootings. It was a blueprint established since the 70's when little Clifford Glover was murdered by police in front of his step-father. The cases of Amadou Diallo, Patrick Dorismond and many more later received the same treatment.

With each case, a new twist is introduced to defend the cops' actions. The Sean Bell case introduced the mysterious fourth man theory. The fourth man must've been the understudy for David Copperfield who managed to wield a gun at cops and was able to pull the greatest magic trick known to man: the disappearing act through a barrage of fifty bullets. I doubt that even Copperfield himself would be able to pull off such a stunt. The NYPD is full of it and I didn't have to write this book to tell you this.

The NYPD somehow wants to forge this ideal reputation with the public and they're willing to go to any length to fabricate something that would take the blame away from them. The hunt for the fourth suspect started with the torment of Sean Bell and his friends' neighbors proving further that the NYPD doesn't give a damn about anybody but themselves. Exoneration at all cost is what they always seek. Their concentration is to try to plant in the public's mind that there was a fourth suspect from the beginning. Raising the stakes by saying that the man was carrying a gun would persuade people to think that maybe the cops had a reason for shooting so many times. It always starts with the court of public opinion so that blames can be deflected from the guilty officers.

It was quite easy for them to start throwing out descriptions of the fourth man to the media immediately after the shooting because most of the young Black men in the hood wear similar clothing. It was said that the fourth man was either near or in the car, which makes absolutely no sense. A fourth man would have had to be down the block to avoid getting shot by the officers' bullets. Even nicknames were thrown to throw the public off. The most disgusting that took place were the raids and hours of interviews, which provided the police with the identification of someone who was the phantom, mystery fourth man five days after the shooting.

The papers reported that the next victim was a 27-year-old man named Jean Nelson who was picked up outside a Jamaica housing complex nicknamed "the Bricks." People were already angry. Clashes between the residents and members of the press who were hoping to get a tip about the fourth suspect made the situation even more tensed. As a police helicopter hovered overhead, angry residents flipped them the bird and cursed at it. Determined officers paraded through the angry crowd and demanded that Nelson come with them.

Attorney Charlie King and the Queens District Attorney forged an agreement that the men wanted for questioning, including Nelson who were with Bell that night, would openly cooperate with their investigation as long as the police would not be involved in a coercion of an illegal statement from the men. King worried that the police would customize their grand jury testimony to the men's statements. He also received a "water-down assurance" from the DA that his clients wouldn't be hassled or intimidated by police. Even the DA understood the length that the police would go through to get a confession or to coerce an untrue statement from witnesses to defend themselves ala Al Capone gang style.

According to published articles, as the detectives neared Nelson, he spotted them and quickly dialed King's telephone number. The attorney asked Nelson to hand the phone to the detective, and told the cop about the agreement with the DA. Nelson was not to talk to the police and the police was to leave his client alone. The phone numbers for the DA and a police supervisor were given to the detective to confirm what he'd been told. Just like a modern street gang, the detective told King "Hold on" to check with his cohorts. And twenty seconds later he was back on the phone telling King, "We're taking him in. We have our orders." "What's the charge?" King asked. Back in gangster mode, the officer answered, "We don't have to tell you that. When King dialed Nelson's number, no one picked up. The police strong armed a witness who had a deal and the police showed total disregard for the district attorney. They wanted to show that they're a gang and the streets of New York City are theirs and no one can tell them what to do except their own.

Police harassment was present from the onset, and King needed to do something quick before it escalated to physical violence against witnesses. The cops in New York are notorious for abuse. Irate about the situation, King quickly placed a call to Testagrossa, the Queens D.A's deputy executive assistant district attorney for major crime to let him have a piece of his mind. "How do you expect people to cooperate with you if you can't assure us that they're going to be free from police harassment?" King asked angrily. No answer was given. The D.A's office knew that the police department is the worst gang that they can ever face in court, so diplomacy had to be used. The DA himself has a spotty record with the Queens community. The imbalance of justice is one that the victims' families are worried about because the DA works closely with the corrupted police departments in Queens.

To eliminate the suspicion of tampering with witnesses, police did not place Nelson under arrest and he wasn't handcuffed as he later told the *Village Voice.* However, he was forced into an unmarked police car against his will and he knew he had better do what he was told because the police department's reputation for violating human rights preceded them.

Nelson was questioned at the station by detectives against his will. "You'll leave in ten minutes and won't have to wait for your lawyer if you tell us what we need," they told him. Nelson was intelligent enough to defer all questions to his lawyer and the cops were finally at their wit's end with him. Finally a lieutenant taunted him when he asked "What do you need a lawyer for if you didn't do anything?" Nelson remained calm and completely avoided the bait the lieutenant threw at him. Nelson was in fact on Liverpool Street the night of the shooting, but he wasn't in close proximity enough to Sean Bell for him to be questioned by the cops as the phantom fourth man.

Finally thirty minutes after he had arrived at the station, the questioning abruptly stopped and Nelson was allowed to go home. King believes it was because the D.A's office had intervened. King admitted to being shocked and appalled at the amount of power the NYPD carried and the way they can use it to cross purposes to investigate the truth. The NYPD misconduct left the Ivy League-educated attorney bewildered. It was business as usual for Nelson because he had grown accustomed to the harassment at the hand of police having grown up in Jamaica, Queens. Game recognized game and to him it was an attempt "to justify what can't be justified."

Of course, the NYPD's chief spokesman, Paul Brown denied that there's ever been a parallel investigation into the case, according to published reports. As he revealed to the Voice that "any arrests after the shooting were purely coincidental," it's interesting that days and weeks prior to the shooting that no one in that community was tormented. Even police Commissioner Kelly told a television reporter, "There hasn't been any stepped up enforcement. That's clear. Any enforcement done in the area is done in the normal course of business. They're always in accord with each other." However, by the time Kelly made his statement, police had conducted many raids and had taken into custody close to ten of Bell's acquaintances. That's what the NYPD wants the people of New York City to believe is the normal course of business.

LaToya Smith, one of the victims of the police raid was afraid for her life, and with good reasons. Police raided her apartment with guns drawn and flashlights in hands. Her seven month old son woke up crying. "I was real scared," she told reporters. A woman who had never been involved with the police and a well-known churchgoer to her community, Latoya was in shock. Unfortunately that raid landed her two brothers in jail when police found a hidden semiautomatic gun. LaToya was released and police questioned her brothers more about Sean Bell than the illegal gun found.

A detective, who spoke with reporters on the condition of anonymity because he's a relative to an officer involved in the case, revealed that the NYPD assigned its entire warrants division, five squads comprising of dozens of cops to the Bell case. "The warrants squad was out there beating the bushes—that's how you get intelligence," said the retired detective, who also added that most of the cops he knows who have worked this case believe this fabricated "Fourth Man Theory." "Somebody's going to have something that they're going to give you. It's basic police work. Saturate the area; you turn the screws a little bit to get more information," information that doesn't exist or is fabricated, most of the time.

Special measures are only taken routinely when egregious or high profile crimes are being solved. However, only when NYPD officers are behind the trigger as opposed to those who do the shooting are such resources made available. It has always been and always will be about protecting their fellow officers no matter whose life is taken. The Most dangerous gang in America wears blue uniforms and carries badges that allows them to take the lives of innocent people and cover it up at all costs. From the lower ranks to the commissioner, many of them are liars and criminals whose badges should be taken away.

4

Alberta Spruill

According to a report by the New York Times on May 17, 2003, titled "Woman Dies After Police Mistakenly Raid Her Apartment" Alberta Spruil, a 57-year-old Harlem woman became a victim of wrong information. She was preparing to leave her home as she usually did every morning for the trek to her longtime city government job when she died of a heart attack during the morning after police officers broke down her door and threw a concussion grenade into her apartment, according to the police commissioner. “They were acting on what appeared to be bad information about guns and drugs in the apartment” police admitted. Commissioner Raymond W. Kelly apologized to the family of the woman, Alberta Spruill, and said he had ordered an investigation of the entire incident and suspended the use of the grenades, which are meant to stun and disorient people with a loud noise and a flash. “I’ve reassigned the lieutenant who made the decision to use the grenade to administrative duties, pending the investigation, and I will review how the grenades were used and search warrants carried out,” Mr. Kelly said. He went on, “the officers were executing what is known as a no-knock search warrant based on information provided by a drug dealer, who told the police that his supplier stored guns and drugs in Apartment 6F at 310 West 143rd Street. The dealer had told the police that he had seen armed people in the apartment on three occasions and that there were dogs inside," Mr. Kelly said. But in the raid at 6:10 a.m., the officers found only Ms. Spruill, and realized the information was wrong and misleading.

The death of Alberta Spruill, resulting from a raid on her apartment by overzealous cops acting on bad information, was ruled a homicide by New York City Police Department's investigators. It was another grave mistake by police and another upstanding citizen's life cut short.

According to the Times, Ms. Spruill, whom relatives and neighbors called hardworking and devout and someone who minded her own business, was a city employee for 29 years. She worked at the Division of Citywide Administrative Services where her duties included maintaining lists of candidates for civil service jobs, including police officers. Mayor Michael R. Bloomberg said that what took place was a tragedy and "a terrible episode," and said in a statement that he joined all city employees in grieving for Ms. Spruill.

The police department's tactics were always questionable, but this time elected official wanted to voice their concerns as well. "Obviously, it's slipshod police work," said State Assemblyman Keith Wright, who added, "I'm sorry to say, but these things happen all too often in this neighborhood." "It did not appear that the drug dealer had given any previous information to the department, although he was registered as a confidential informant," said police commissioner Kelly at a news conference a few hours after Ms. Spruill's death. He also went on to say "it was unclear whether the officers involved in the raid, who were from the 25th Precinct, conducted any surveillance of the building or the apartment before executing the search warrant, which was signed by Judge Patricia M. Nunez of Criminal Court."

5

Ousmane Zongo

Ousmane Zongo was a forty-three-year-old Burkinabé arts trader who fixed African artifacts for a living in the Chelsea section of Manhattan. He was a quiet hard working man who cared greatly for his family back home in Burkina, Faso. He was the breadwinner for his family. Zongo was killed by a plainclothes cop on May 22, 2003, after being chased through a hallway inside a Chelsea storage facility. Police never identified themselves and only responded with their service revolvers. Feared for his life and in the dark about his situation, Zongo ran for safety, but he couldn't escape the bullets of the murderous cop who aimed to kill him that day. Hours after the fatal shooting, it was business as usual when the police ransacked his Morningside Heights apartment and took two of his roommates in for six hours of questioning about Zongo, a third roommate said.

The deceiving methods that the NYPD use after killing innocent victims must be exposed and investigated. The level of corruption within the police department is a great danger to civilians and the officers understand that they're backed by a corrupted system that will defend them or even plant evidence if necessary to prove their innocence even when they are guilty. Ousmane Zongo's death is just a drop in the bucket, there have been more and there will continue to be more.

The officer, Bryan Conroy, involved in the shooting death of Ousmane Zongo only received probation in court. Bryan Conroy was found guilty of criminal negligent homicide. The judge who oversaw the case placed blame on the improper training of police officers by the NYPD. However, his family reached a settlement with the City of New York for three million dollars. Zongo's and Ms. Spruil's shootings were days apart.

6

Malcolm Ferguson

A couple of weeks before Patrick Dorismond was unjustly shot to death in March 2000; another undercover officer executed another unarmed Black man at point-blank range in the Bronx. Malcolm Ferguson, 25, was shot in the head after cops chased him through a building in the Bronx as part of the anti-drug blitz. He had filed a civil lawsuit against New York City and its Police Department over an earlier arrest where cops broke his hand and left him without medical attention. Neighbors, friend and family suggested that he may have been executed for seeking legal action against police brutality. I know it sounds like I'm writing a book on the Crips and Bloods, but it's actually the police department of New York City that is supposed to protect and serve the people.

Ferguson had been arrested just a week before for participating in a protest over the acquittal of Diallo's police killers. The New York City police Department retaliated against this man by taking his life away.

According to an article written in the *Village Voice*, Malcolm Ferguson had every reason to be afraid and cautious of police. He was about a month shy of completing his parole for a heroin-selling conviction, and his attorney was near filing a $5 million brutality suit against the city, accusing police of breaking his hand while handcuffing him during a March 9, 1999, drug arrest.

As the protest started to slowly die down, Ferguson and other protesters were trying to board a bus, according to a friend named Libby. “The bus driver just told him to get off,” Libby recalls. That’s when cops grabbed Ferguson. A *Fox 5 TV* camera captured the arrest and showed Ferguson grimacing, his face pressed against the roadway, as he was being handcuffed behind his back ruthlessly by police. Ferguson, who wore baggy jeans that sagged to expose plaid boxer shorts and an unzipped jacket, was then hoisted and escorted hurriedly by plainclothes cops to a police van. He was charged with disorderly conduct and resisting arrest. May his life serve a purpose to other people and hopefully his soul will rest in peace.

7

Patrick Dorismond

Just a few days after the shooting death of Malcolm Ferguson, the New York City police officers were up to their old tricks again. Another highly publicized shooting of an unarmed Black man by the name of Patrick Dorismond was making the headlines this time. Dorismond was shot and killed by an NYPD police officer in the Manhattan section of New York City. Twenty-six-year-old Dorismond worked as a security guard to take care of his family. He was shot to death on March 15, 2000 by plainclothes officers involved in a controversial anti-drug crackdown. There was no clear evidence that Dorismond knew that the man who pulled a gun on him and shot him with a single bullet to his chest was a police officer.

Dorismond was the father of two young girls who had dreams of becoming a cop himself in New York City. He and his friend were confronted by an undercover cop outside of a bar in lower Manhattan. While trying to hail a cab to get home, the police officer approached him asking to purchase drugs. Police claimed Dorismond became belligerent. Backup officers were called as well as plainclothes officer, Detective Anthony Vasquez. The New York Police Department's version of the event had the security guard throwing a punch at the officers for no reason at all, and Vasquez's attorney claimed that his client's gun went off after Dorismond was trying to steal it from him. However, eyewitnesses gave drastically different accounts of what happened.

Dorismond was a completely innocent victim of aggressive police behavior towards black men. Dorismond had no idea that the men who confronted and then killed him were police officers. He was offended that someone assumed he was a drug dealer because of his age and his race and he reacted in a way that the police disapprove and felt warranted his death.

Again, the old NYPD tactics reappear to taint the victim's name as he lay dead in a morgue. The NYPD didn't even wait for his burial before the lead gang member at the time, Rudy Giuliani, came out swinging and slinging mud at the man's name. Giuliani quickly directed that Dorismond's sealed juvenile record for a robbery over a fight when he was a teenager, be released to the public. He also went on the record to say that Dorismond was "no altar boy." It turned out that he had indeed been an altar boy to Giuliani's ignorance. Police also searched his family's home, infuriating the victim's family more during their moment of grief in an attempt to defend the murderous cops once again.

8

Amadou Diallo

Published accounts of the events surrounding the death of Amadou Diallo painted a picture of a young man in pursuit of the American dream. The barbaric, Iraqi firing squad-style killing of Amadou Diallo was only part of a systemic abuse of badge, gun and oath by New York City police officers in February 1999 when his life was taken.

Amadou Diallo was born on September 2, 1975 in the village of Sinoe, Liberia, West Africa. He was the first of four children born to Saikou and Kadiatou Diallo. Amadou has one sister, Laouratou, and two brothers, Ibrahima and Abdul Salaam. Amadou traveled throughout much of his childhood living in Togo, Guinea, the homeland of his parents, Bangkok and Singapore due to the fact that his father, Saikou, was a businessman.

As a youngster, Amadou had a voracious appetite and love for reading, music, dancing and sports. Soon after his arrival in the United States, he became an avid basketball fan, and like most true basketball fans, he loved Michael Jordan. The Chicago Bulls could've won the NBA championship every year while Jordan played for them and it would've been fine with Amadou. He also had a passion for school and attended some of the finest schools in the world, including The French International School, London's Cambridge University, The British Consulate College in Thailand and the Asian Institute of Microsoft. It was his dream to also attend school in the United States in the future, but there would be no future. Completely removing himself from the grasp of his parents, Diallo decided to move to America to continue his computer education at the young age of twenty years old because he wanted to do it on his own. He moved to New York in September 1996 to start a business with his cousin. His father, Saikou, was never comfortable with the idea that his son wanted to live in New York, but he eventually eased off after relatives in the States promised to look after Amadou and keep him safe.

Shortly after his arrival in New York, he worked as a delivery man. Unsatisfied with his earnings and the lack of opportunity in his position, he decided to become an entrepreneur, selling gloves, socks and video tapes in Manhattan on 14th Street. He worked six days a week, and long twelve hour days. He was determined to realize his dream of an education in America. Amadou was passionate about education. He wanted to one day enroll at one of the universities in America, but that dream would be cut short by nineteen bullets.

Amadou was also a very spiritual man. At the age of eighteen, he started to focus on his Islamic religion as well as collect books about Islam to further help him understand the foundation of his belief. He studied the Koran and prayed five times a day in the Muslim tradition. Amadou was on a spiritual journey. His parents couldn't be more proud when they arrived to New York to pick up his belongings and discovered that he had not lost his discipline, determination and drive as a person as well as his belief in Islam.

On February 4, 1999, after midnight, Amadou Diallo would see his last day as he was unjustly killed by four white New York City police officers from the "Street Crime Unit." After a long working day, Amadou went to his apartment at 1157 Wheeler Avenue in the Soundview Section of the Bronx. It was there he decided to go back out to get something to munch on. However, on his way back to the house, he encountered the four police officers who ultimately took his life when they fired a barrage of 41 shots, 19 of which pierced through his body. Amadou died in the lobby of his apartment. He was only a few steps from entering the safety of his home. However, the determination of the officers to pull the trigger prevented him from doing just that.

In the aftermath after the shooting death of Amadou Diallo by the NYPD, they were back to their old tricks again. Police searched the tiny apartment of the African Immigrant that he shared with roommates, turning over beds and pulling out drawers. Diallo's cousin, Abdourahmane Diallo and another roommate were quickly taken into custody and questioned for several hours about Diallo's legal status in the States and his background. Police even kept the fact that they had killed Diallo from his cousin and acted as if they were investigating whether he had enemies or not. They also scoured Diallo's past for a criminal record, but none was found. With their backs against the wall, the NYPD decided to reveal Diallo's immigration status to the media in an attempt to paint him as a liar who lied on his immigration application to gain asylum in the United States. He lost his life because the cops mistook his wallet for a gun. They were trying to get any kind of information to build a case against a dead man and defend one of their own.

It's disturbing how this pattern of behavior has gone unnoticed and the most corrupted police department continues to operate as if they're immune from the law: and that taking the lives of minority folks only warrant a suspension or a transfer to desk duties.

9

Abner Louima

The brutality at the hands of the police didn't start with just Abner Louima in 1997, but that was the year that I moved to New York City in search of my big dream as a stand-up comic and a writer. I will also touch upon the strangling death of Anthony Baez in December of 1994 at the hand of rogue cops in this book and many other defenseless victims. Louima's case evokes a different type of emotion from me because I lived in New York when it happened. Abner Louina's case was the first time since the lynching of Black men during the early nineteenth century that I had heard about such a heinous crime against a black man by police officers in a major city where I resided. There have been hundreds of unarmed victims that died at the hand of police, but to keep this in perspective, I'm only talking about most of the ones that took place since I've lived in New York.

Abner Louima became a victim of police torture when he got arrested outside of a nightclub in Brooklyn in 1997. He was handcuffed and taken to Brooklyn's 70th precinct. Then 30-year-old Louima was married and had two children with his wife, and had been living in Brooklyn for the past six years. Trained as an electrical engineer in his homeland of Haiti, Louima, worked as a security guard in a water and sewage plant in Flatlands, Brooklyn. Louima visited "Club Rendez-Vous", a popular nightclub in East Flatbush, Brooklyn on August 9th, 1997. Sometime late during the night, Louima and a few other men tried to stop a fight between two women in the club. A fight ensued and the police were called and dispatched to the scene from the 70th precinct. Soon after their arrival, a confrontation between the police and the clubgoers and onlookers evolved into a scuffle outside the club. The responding officers included, Justin Volpe, Charles Schwarz, Thomas Bruder, Thomas Wiese, and a few others. In the ensuing brawl, officer Volpe thought he was hit by what he called a "sucker-punch" and for reasons unknown to the media and the rest of his corp of officers, he identified Louima as the sucker puncher. Louima was arrested on charges of disorderly conduct, obstructing government administration, and resisting arrest by Officer Volpe.

While in police custody, Louima was beaten with fists, nightsticks, and handheld radios by the arresting officers on the way to the station. After arriving to the police station, he was strip searched and put in a jail cell. The beatings would continue later while a staff sergeant was on duty. Louima was kicked in the groin, sodomized with a plunger while his hands were in handcuffs behind his back by then police officer Justin Volpe. Volpe was not alone in his abuse against Louima, Officers Weise, Schwartz and Bruder assisted in the abuse. The assault by the law enforcement officers included the shoving of a wooden broomstick into Louima's rectum tearing a one inch hole in his rectum, and causing severe damage to his colon and bladder. The same broomstick was also shoved in his mouth causing great damage to his teeth. Louima needed several surgeries to repair the damage to his torn bladder and intestine.

Louima was transferred to the Coney Island Hospital emergency room the day after the incident. The officers who escorted Mr. Louima to the hospital explained away his serious injuries being a result of "abnormal homosexual activities." Once again, officers started lying to cover their crime. Sometimes we have to wonder who the real criminals are in New York City. Fortunately for Louima, a fellow Haitian emergency room nurse named Magalie Laurent was on duty that day. Suspiscious that the nature of Louima's extreme injuries were not the result of gay sex, she notified Louima's family and the Police Department's Internal Affairs Bureau of the likelihood of sexual assault and battery. Louima remained hospitalized two months thereafter to recover.

Abner Louima was one of the lucky few victims who didn't perish at the hands of police ofiicers while in their custody. God bless him and I hope he always takes part in the crusade against police brutality. After all, what is the purpose of a man if he stands for nothing? Louima's case should have prompted the NYPD to change the procedure used to screen potential police applicants. However, none of that mattered because the victim was a black man.

10

Nathaniel Levi Gaines Jr.

Parallel investigation in New York City is routine, and has been for over thirty years. On July 24, 1996 a 25–year-old navy veteran of the first Gulf war by the name of Nathaniel Levi Gaines Jr. was shot and killed execution style by Officer Paolo Colecchia on a subway platform in the Bronx. Colecchia started his defense mechanism for why he pulled the trigger moments after the shooting. He made several claims that Gaines had a gun; Gaines was a stalker, stalking a feared woman; Gaines attempted to throw him on the tracks. As Colecchia tried to put together the pieces of his botched story, his fellow compadres were digging up dirt on Gaines trying to build a case to justify the shooting.

Police officers checked out his job with The New York State Thruway Authority where he worked as a toll taker, they questioned his co-workers, and turned up every leaf they could find. The NYPD were so busy looking for dirt on the victim, they failed to notify his parents of his death. Unfortunately, a reporter had to deliver the bad news when he was seeking comment on the questionable shooting.

Unbeknownst to Colecchia, a witness had seen him shoot Gaines in the back while he ran down the subway platform. "They tried all sorts of things to cover it up," the victim's stepmother, Mary Gaines, told the *Voice*. "We immediately knew it was all a bunch of lies. That's just the way they do things." She said Gaines's father, Nathaniel Sr., who served in Vietnam, died 14 months after his son's death. Nathaniel Sr. was stricken with cancer, the wife said, but his son's death drained him of his will to fight it. "You don't want to know how something like this destroys a family," she said. She knew all too well what the public didn't know about the NYPD cover-ups.

11

Anthony Baez

Anthony Baez was killed by a New York police officer for allowing his football to strike officer Livotti's patrol car. That was a crime Anthony Baez paid for with his life. Anthony Baez was a young man with dreams. According to an interview given by his father, Ramon Baez, Anthony and his wife planned to have a family. He was working two jobs and going to college. He was trying to improve his life. A cold-blooded murderer took all of it away and he wore a uniform, carried a badge and a gun that's supposed to protect and serve. This crime was committed in plain view of many witnesses. Officer Livotti was out for blood.

As reported, it was the Christmas holiday in 1994. The Baez family came together as a tradition every year to celebrate the birth of Christ. A few members came up from Florida to see their close relatives, but it was time to go back home. Worried about all the traffic they might encounter, they decided to leave very early in the morning. Everything was packed except for the people themselves who were leaving. There was some time to kill, so they decided to spend it with the family. The energy was high while the family played a few rounds of cards around one o'clock in the morning, according to the elder Mr. Baez's account of the events to a newspaper. It was then that the four Baez brothers decided to go outside to play a game of touch football. Iris Baez was always pleased to have her children play in front of her house so she could watch them. The Baez clan was having fun throwing the football around…then suddenly the brother playing quarterback was not so accurate with his pass. The ball hit the roof of a police car parked on the street. It was no big deal. An apology was offered.

That street was one of the streets that the cops favored when they wanted to sit back, relax, eat doughnuts and drink coffee. They referred to it as "anti-crime work", but since there was no crime, how exactly were they working? The truth of the matter was that it was cops doing whatever they damn well pleased. Suddenly, another cop car pulled up with super cop, Francis Livoti, behind the wheel. A cop with a maligned record of 14 official complaints filed against him by civilians ranging from choking to harassment. He's accompanied by a sergeant who was supposed to be monitoring him to prevent further improper conduct. Thud...another pass was thrown off course, the ball hit Livoti's car this time around. He immediately ordered the Baez brothers to go home after stepping out of his car. However, they were already home. No backyard in the back of their building and confined to the walls of their parents' apartment most of the day, they tried to continue their game. Livotti was enraged because his orders had not been followed. "That's it! Who wants to fight?" he yelled with an obvious temper. All hell started breaking loose and Livotti went after David, one of the brothers, and arrested him. As most siblings would have done, Anthony came to his brother's aide by protesting the arrest. The officer became agitated and more enraged and turned on Anthony with his famous chokehold that's been on his blemished record for years. Anthony, a guy who toppled over Livotti and an ex-wrestler, chose not to inflict any pain on the officer. He never resisted, but the choking continued. Livotti was enraged with anger as he pressed harder against Anthony's neck for more than a minute to choke the living life out of him in front of his family.

Anthony's lifeless body was dangling in the officer's hands as his family pleaded for the officer to stop hurting their son. His father abruptly came to the scene yelling "he has asthma." Officer Livotti turned to him in a mocking tone and yelled back, "He has asthma!" Livotti yells back, "He's sick? He has asthma? Good for him." After the officer finally let him go, Anthony's body hit the ground as he fell unconscious on his face in the middle of the street. Livotti placed his knee on Anthony's back as enforcement while he handcuffed the dead man. Anthony's lifeless body lay on the ground for fifteen minutes before they dragged him to a police car. He died in front of his family. His family was screaming, "He has asthma...don't hurt him...somebody call the cops!" One of the cops yelled back, "We are the cops, you idiots!" They called the parents of a man they just murdered idiots.

12

Clifford Glover

Initially, I only intended to focus on the most recent shootings that took place in New York City by the NYPD, but I feel that it is also important to highlight the history of these violent incidents by NYPD police officers. This has been going on since the sixties and nobody is safe. Even young children have been murdered and then their names smeared after their death.

The NYPD has always managed to fool the public into thinking that they're New York's finest. I guess if you're thinking about New York's finest criminals, you might be right. The NYPD's reputation is what it's always been about. On April 28, 1973, Clifford Glover, a five foot, 98 pound, 10-year-old, was shot in the back while running away from Officer Thomas Shea in not so surprisingly South Jamaica, Queens. It was one of the most notorious murders of a kid at the hands of a police officer.

A taxi driver had reported that he was robbed by two individuals. While looking for the suspects, Shea encountered the boy and his stepfather, Add Armstead, who were on their way to Mr. Armstead's job at a junkyard. The man was on his way to work to earn a living to support his family. According to Shea, the 10-

year-old boy fired a shot at him as he approached the stepfather and son. Shea also claimed he returned fire striking the boy, who then took off running. However, before falling with the bullet in his body, the boy was somehow able to pass the gun off to his stepfather, claimed Shea.

Even then frenetic parallel investigations were being conducted on behalf of criminal cops. Patrolmen from the 103rd Precinct reviewed files at the Queens County Narcotics Bureau hoping to find Add Armstead's name, Eloise Glover, the boy's mother or Clifford Glover, the shooting victim. This case was also documented in another book called The Trial Of Patrolman Thomas Shea by Thomas Hauser. Investigators came up empty after searching, but they were not done yet. To vilify the family, the police pursued a tip from an "anonymous source" who reported that the real Clifford Glover died shortly after birth and that the child shot by the officer was illegally shipped to New York by a relative of Eloise Glover for Welfare purposes.

Through all their futile efforts, investigators could not find anything, but a police union trustee urged the investigating cops to press on because something was bound to come up to substantiate Shea's claim. The police Union in New York continue to be a hindrance to justice as they continue to pressure investigating officers to look for non-existing evidence in fatal cases just as they're pressing for evidence to show that Sean Bell was somehow criminally connected or associated.

It appears that while police officers continue to beat their truth out of witnesses they continue to overlook their own pattern of lies in New York City to dignify a police department that has a long history of undercutting its citizens through vicious lies and made up fibs to clear their path of destruction.

The practice of parallel investigation by the NYPD should receive scrutiny from the Federal Justice Department and those found to be part of witness tampering and other illegal violations of the law should be punished to the full extent of the law. Until something is done about this, New Yorkers will continue to live in a city where the police operate as a street gang and they will stop at nothing to get the justice that they want and deem fit.

13

More National Victims of Police Shootings

The New Jersey Turnpike, New Jersey, four young men were riding in a van on the New Jersey Turnpike, three black and one Latino in April 1998 when they were stopped by two New Jersey state troopers. They were on their way to a university basketball try-out. The van accidentally rolled backwards, causing an officer to fall over. The police officers opened fire, and three of the young men sustained multiple gunshot wounds without ever being fired upon. The officers said they had stopped the vehicle for speeding, but the men denied that they were ever speeding and claimed they had been targeted because of their race. One of the troopers involved in the shooting had been involved in at least 19 prior incidents in which it was alleged he had stopped vehicles because of the occupants' race. It took 19 incidents and a hail of bullets before this officer was disciplined.

Columbus, Georgia, Kenneth B. Walker, a 39-year-old father and husband was shot and killed by police when Walker and three companions were pulled over in an SUV by police in a drug investigation. No drugs or weapons were found, but Walker was shot in the head. Walker was a devoted husband and father, a respected member of his church, and a 15-year middle-management employee of Blue Cross and Blue Shield.

According to the Banner-Herald, Walker and three friends were pulled over in their gray GMC Yukon on a Wednesday night. Officers with guns drawn ordered the four men, "Get on the ground! Get on the ground! Get on the ground! Let me see your hands!" Walker's three companions apparently complied with the commands, but Walker provided "some resistance," according to the sheriff's account. Although Walker was on the ground, his right hand couldn't be seen by the officers, Johnson said. The deputy fired at least two shots, including the fatal shot to Walker's head. No gun was found in the Yukon. Walker died during surgery about 2:25 a.m. Thursday. The other three men were released.

St. Louis, MO, it was the summer of 2000 when **Ronald Beasley** found himself in the wrong place at the wrong time. For whatever reason, Beasley accepted a ride from Earl Murray, a known small-time dope dealer to police. Murray stopped at a fast-food restaurant on North Hanley Road, where he had previously agreed to meet a guy who wanted to buy some dope from him without saying anything to Beasley. The buyer was an undercover cop who was well aware of Murray, and when his colleagues moved in to arrest Murray, Murray panicked and tried to drive away. However, two of the cops were afraid that Murray was going to run into them, and so they panicked. A barrage of bullets was discharged and Murray and Beasley were each hit multiple times and killed.

Nothing much was released about the case. Murray and Beasley were both unarmed at the time of the incident. It was revealed that Murray had sold small amounts of drugs to the undercover agents on two other occasions. Only a quarter of an ounce of cocaine was found in Murray's car at the time of his and Beasley's death. Beasley was not wanted for anything.

Annette Green was killed when *St. Louis, MO*, County police officers smashed in her door for a drug bust. As they entered her house, Ms. Green suddenly appeared at the top of the stairs when she heard the noise. According to her family, she was holding a phone. The police version was that she had a bolt in her hand, and as she descended the stairs, an officer, aiming through the beams of the flashlights, shot and killed her because he felt his life was threatened by a woman standing away from him. The cops said a small amount of drugs was found in the home. Two juveniles and four men were in the house.

Inglewood, California July 2002, a videotaped incident showing a police officer, Jeremy Morse, smashing the face of a handcuffed Black teenager, ***Donovan Jackson***, into the hood of a police cruiser and then punching him in the face was nationally televised to show the abusive behavior that police display towards black men.

LEBANON, Tennessee – it was reported About ten o'clock in the evening on a Wednesday in October 2006, 64-year-old ***John Adams***, settled into his tan recliner to watch television for the last time, his cane within easy reach in case he needed to get up for whatever reason. However, John Adams would never get up again and his cane would remain near his lifeless body where he last rested in his home.

While John Adams enjoyed a leisure moment in his own domain, Lebanon police officers, 25-year-old Kyle Shedran, and 24-year-old Greg Day, stood armed at his door and prepared for the worst. In the darkness, five to seven other officers were also there for backup. Shedran and Day knocked. Adams' wife, Loriane, 61, moved to the door to see who it was. In the next moment, everyone's lives changed forever, victims of a horrendous mistake. "It was a severe, costly mistake," Lebanon Police Chief Billy Weeks said at an afternoon news conference the day after. "They were not the target of our investigation. We hate that it happened."

By then John Adams had been dead more than 12 hours, shot to death by Shedran and Day after they said, Adams shot at them with a sawed-off shotgun. Friends and relatives said John Adams believed it was a home invasion when police kicked in the door after refusing to identify themselves. "They made a mistake, and he was trying to defend his home, and they shot him," said Edward Bell, Adams' nephew. The problem is that those mistakes are only common in the Black community where everything can go wrong.

Others were not prepared to offer even a hint of understanding. “They murdered my best friend," said former Wilson County Commissioner Natchel Palmer. “They got the wrong damn house and killed my friend.” Police details of what happened in the Adams' house were unavailable to the public and the little that was released was very sketchy at best.

Cincinnati, Ohio, the beleaguered police department beat to death *Nathaniel Jones* in Cincinnati, the 18th Black man to be killed by police in that city since 1995.

Atlanta, Georgia, 8-year-old *Xavier Bennett* was accidentally shot to death by officers in a pre-dawn drug raid during a gunfight with one of Xavier's relatives.

Belpre, Ohio, 57-year-old *Delbert Bonnar* was shot 8 times in October 1998 by police during a drug raid. They were looking for his son, but he was killed instead.

San Jose, California, *Rudolfo "Rudy" Cardenas*, a 43-year-old man was shot multiple times in the back February, 2004. Rudy was a father of five who was passing by a house targeted by narcotics officers attempting to serve a parole violation warrant and the police mistakenly thought he was the one they were there to arrest. They chased Cardenas, and he fled, apparently afraid of them (they were not uniformed). Dorothy Duckett, 78, told the Mercury News she looked out her fifth-floor window after hearing one gunshot and saw Cardenas pleading for his life. "I watched him running with his hands in the air. He kept saying, 'Don't shoot. Don't shoot,'" Duckett said. "He had absolutely nothing in his hands."

Anthony Andrew Diotaiuto, 23 years old from *Sunrise, Florida* was killed in August, 2005. Anthony worked two jobs to help pay for the house he lived in with his mother. He had a permit for a concealed weapon because of the areas he traveled through for his night job. Sunrise police claimed that he had sold some marijuana, and because they knew he had a legal gun, decided to use SWAT. Neighbors claim that the police did not identify themselves. Police first claimed that Anthony pointed his gun at them, and later changed their story. Regardless, Anthony was dead with 10 bullets in him, and the police found 2 ounces of marijuana. Two ounces of marijuana is enough to get a person of color killed.

Juan Mendoza Fernandez, 60 years old from *Dallas, Texas* was shot while trying to protect his 11-year-old granddaughter on September, 2000. Police found a variety of drugs when they raided the Fernandez' home. However, Juan apparently believed he was the victim of burglars during the raid. He and his wife had been married 36 years and had four children and 13 grandchildren. Another warrant gone badly and a grandfather taken...

Curt Ferryman, 24 years old from *Jacksonville, Florida* was killed in August, 2000. Undercover agents were attempting to arrest Ferryman, who was in his car and unarmed. A DEA agent knocked on the car window with his gun to get the suspect's attention, and the gun went off, killing him as he sat in the car.

Willie Heard, 46 years old from *Osawatomie, Kansas* was killed in February, 1999 SWAT conducted a no-knock drug raid, complete with flash-bang grenades. Heard was shot to death in front of his wife and 16-year-old daughter who had cried for help. Fearing home invasion, he was holding an empty rifle. The raid was at the wrong house and they killed an innocent victim.

Lynette Gayle Jackson, 29 years old from *Riverdale,*

Georgia was shot to death in her bed by SWAT team in September, 2000. Her life was cut short during a raid.

Tony Marinez, 19 years old from *De Valle, Texas* was killed in December, 2001. Officers were conducting a drug raid on a mobile home in De Valle, Martinez, who was not the target of the raid, was asleep on the couch when the raid commenced. Hearing the front door smashed open, he sat up to see what was happening, and was shot to death in the chest by cops.

Manuel Ramirez from *Stockton, California* was killed in January, 1993. At 2 am, police smashed down the door and rushed into the home of Manuel Ramirez, a retired golf course groundskeeper. Ramirez awoke, grabbed a pistol and shot and killed Officer Arthur Parga before other officers killed him. Police were raiding the house based on a tip that drugs were on the premises, but they found no drugs.

Gary Shepherd, 45 years old from *Broadhead, Kentucky* was killed in August, 1993. When a Kentucky drug task force came to uproot his marijuana plants in August 1993, pot-grower and Vietnam vet Gary Shepherd told them, "You will have to kill me first," took out his rifle and sat down on his front porch. That evening he was shot dead in front of his infant son. Despite the fact that Shepherd never fired a shot and his family was pleading with authorities for negotiations, state police sharpshooters appeared from the brush without warning and opened fire when he refused to drop his rifle to the ground.

Accelyne Williams, 75 years old from *Boston, Massachusetts* was killed in March, 1994. Williams was a retired Methodist Minister and substance abuse counselor. After an informant gave police a bad address, a SWAT raid was conducted on the minister's home. The door was battered down, Williams was tackled to the floor and his hands tied behind his back. He died of a heart attack as officers ignored his condition.

As a Suffolk police helicopter hovered overhead at 862 Doane Avenue in *Suffolk County, Long Island, New York*, at least eight heavily armed officers of the well known Elite Emergency Services unit were swarming on the same address, 20-year-old, *Jose Colon* had no idea that it would be his last day alive. He was at the house to repay a debt, friends and relatives said, when police raided the single-story blue-paneled house suspected of being a drug den. His pregnant girlfriend sat in a car 20 to 30 feet away as she watched in horror when he was shot once in the head by police.

Colon was shot as he emerged from the house. Unbeknownst to him was the fact that the house under investigation for drugs and was being raided by the cops. Officers said the raid turned deadly when an officer carrying a battering ram tripped on a tree root, bumping into the lead officer, causing both to fall to the ground. As the first officer fell he accidentally fired three shots, one fatally wounding Colon. Another accident and mistake by police left another innocent man dead. Another grave mistake by police.

Family members said Jose stayed away from trouble, worked hard and enjoyed the computer. He was a senior at Briarcliffe College where he excelled in computer graphics. "This is a nightmare, I can't stop shaking. I can't believe they killed my brother," his sister said. Another promising young life cut short prematurely.

LEWISBURG, Ohio – According to published reports, a tip from an informant about marijuana trafficking led Preble County authorities to send the sheriff's emergency services unit on a surprise drug raid to a rural farmhouse on Sept. 27, 2002 Sheriff Tom Hayes said. Those tips seemed to be the latest reasons why a lot of raids have gone haywire in the last few years. Police have not improved their system to make sure tips are valid before risking innocent lives.

The specially trained police squad rarely is assigned to serve a search warrant, Hayes said. But the previous week, Preble County sheriff's commanders had learned that more than a dozen men might be at the home, so they sent the emergency services unit. The unit's 15 members are equipped to handle drownings, water rescues, and hostage and other high-risk situations. One of the primary mistakes made in this raid was obviously sending the wrong people to serve a warrant. We have to wonder about the precautionary measures the police departments used when it comes to black life. It's almost nonsensical and careless on their part when they're dealing with minority folks. No emphasis is placed on accuracy. Whatever resource they have at their disposal can be used regardless of the threat and danger it may pose to black people's lives.

Minutes after the officers forced their way into ***Clayton J. Helriggle's*** rented farmhouse outside of ***West Alexandria, in Ohio***, a Lewisburg police sergeant assigned to the group shot and killed the 23-year-old man as he walked down a flight of stairs.

The officer, 41-year-old Sgt. Kent Moore, has been placed on administrative leave while Montgomery County sheriff's officers investigate Helriggle's death, Lewisburg Police Chief John Wright said. "He is in seclusion," Wright said. "Naturally, he's taking it very hard." Imagine how hard the victim's family must be taking it. At least, the shooting officer can still be around for his family. It must not have been that hard for him to pull the trigger. With all his training he made the biggest mistake of taking someone's life.

Moore, a Lewisburg police officer since 1983, also is a certified weapons instructor who serves as a sheriff's deputy when the Preble County emergency services unit is activated. It's always great to list the special trainings that these officers have, but when it comes time to apply their training it seems that all the training and caution are thrown out the window.

The Preble County sheriff said the raid was an unusual assignment for his office's emergency services unit. If it was so unusual, what was the rush? Why couldn't they wait to properly handle the situation with the right personnel? Again, another case of blatant disrespect for a human life by police officers.

"Most of the time, we don't even use them on the search warrants," the chief said. "It all depends on what it is." He said a three-day investigation into allegations of marijuana trafficking at the Lanier Twp. Farmhouse where Helriggle and four others lived included "intelligence they gathered" and information from an unidentified informant who said "an estimated dozen or more people" would be at the farmhouse September 27, 2002. Those people didn't deserve to die.

"That's what made it a little more high risk. You gotta be careful on something like that," Hayes said. The risks must not have outweighed the right choice. Eaton Municipal Judge Paul Henry approved a search warrant earlier on Sept. 27. That Monday, he ordered it sealed until the investigation is complete. Helriggle, who worked for his family's business, Helriggle Garage Doors, had a routine, said Sharon Helriggle, his mother. "He'd work, go home, work out, take a shower and take a nap," she said. Then friends would come to the farmhouse for a night of guitar playing, movies, playing games in the back of the farm and relaxing. Drinking beer and smoking marijuana was part of their routine, Helriggle's mother said. "There were easily 15 to 18 of them here, sometimes more," Helriggle's father, Michael, said.

Police returned to the farmhouse Sept. 28 to execute the search warrant. Officers seized a small amount of marijuana, pipes and a bong, papers used in rolling the drug, and weapons, according to a Preble County sheriff's incident report written that Wednesday.

Also found in the house "in close proximity to the body," Hayes said, was a 9 mm handgun owned by Helriggle. That gun, which friends said Helriggle kept in his room, is at the heart of the disagreement between police and Helriggle's roommates and relatives. The roommates and relatives say Helriggle had a plastic cup full of water - not a gun - in his hand when he walked down dimly lit stairs before Moore shot him in the chest once with a shotgun. Two different versions of a story were told about a mistaken death.

According to the sheriff's report, members of the emergency services unit entered the house, and two officers shot at three dogs. Three roommates were subdued and another, Helriggle, was encountered coming down the stairs with a gun, according to the report.

One of the roommates, Ian Arnold, said Helriggle walked downstairs after being awakened from a nap and carried only a blue plastic cup. "I don't know what cup they're talking about," Hayes said a few days after the shooting when he had time to think.

In a report published in The Atlanta Journal Constitution, Atlanta police carelessly shot and killed a 92-year-old retired senior citizen in her home in ***Atlanta, Georgia*** during a botched raid intended to find a well-known coke dealer. Cynthia Tucker of the Atlanta Journal-Constitution wrote on Dec. 4, 2006 wrote in an article titled "88-Year-Old Woman Is Latest Collateral Damage In Senseless Drug War" ***Kathryn Johnston*** was collateral damage in America's misguided "war on drugs." Johnston was actually 92 years old. The report went on to say that on Nov. 21, 2006 the 92-year-old woman was shot dead by Atlanta undercover police officers who crashed through her door after dark to execute a "no-knock" search warrant for illegal drugs. Living in a high-crime neighborhood, apparently frightened the elderly woman out of her wits, so she fired at the intruders with a rusty revolver, hitting all three as they crashed through her door. These are the events that took place according to police. Ms. Johnston was killed when fire was returned and she was hit in the chest and extremities. From the beginning there were signs of police improprieties in the case. The FBI as well as the Georgia Bureau of Investigation (GBI) were asked to review the actions of the narcotics officers by Police Chief Richard Pennington. The investigation revealed police deception, incompetence, and police malfeasance. As it always has been, it is very difficult to point to the root cause of tragedies such as this. The police department's effort to curb the use of illegal drugs has been fruitless. The "war on drugs" has caused an insurmountable amount of deaths in the Black community - leaving children fatherless, helping to bitterly increase the spread of AIDS, and babysitting in prisons mostly the less fortunate people who, with the help of counseling and rehabilitation, might be contributing to society instead of being part of a new industry dubbed "slave labor" behind bars.

The incident was questionable at best. The Atlanta Journal-Constitution reported on Nov. 27, 2006 in an article titled, "Informant In Shooting Says He Never Bought Drugs At Home" The confidential informant whose word call for the Atlanta police raid, said he never purchased any drugs from the victim's house, and was told by police to lie and say he did. Chief Richard Pennington, in a press conference the following Monday evening, said "The informant said he had no knowledge of going into that house and purchasing drugs. We don't know if he's telling the truth." The informant had always maintained that he did not provide information to officers about a drug deal at 933 Neal Street in northwest Atlanta. The search warrant used by Atlanta police to raid the house says that a confidential informant had bought crack cocaine at the residence, using $50 in city funds, several hours before the raid. In the document, officers lied and said that the informant told them the house had surveillance cameras that the suspected drug dealer, called "Sam," monitored. Kathryn Johnston had no cameras in her home and no drugs. All she wanted to do was to safeguard her residence and live the rest of her life peacefully. She managed to escape the rough streets of northwest Atlanta most of her life, but tragically her life was violently taken by those who are supposed to protect her. Pennington that Monday evening said "the informant told the Internal Affairs Unit that he did not tell officers that the house had surveillance equipment, and that he was asked to lie." It appears to be another case of parallel investigation, and coercion by police to cover their tracks. These gung ho officers don't value black life enough to ensure accuracy of "gathered intelligence."

Ms. Johnston's family will finally have peace as the officers who killed her have been indicted on many different charges. According to an April 26th report in the Atlanta Journal Constitution, three Atlanta police narcotics officers involved in the botched drug raid that killed the elderly woman in her northwest Atlanta home have been indicted by a Fulton County grand jury. The indictments, reached late Wednesday, April 25, 2007 were announced Thursday morning. The officers are Gregg Junnier, Arthur Tesler and Jason R. Smith. Details of the indictment were not immediately available.

Guilty pleas on state charges and federal charges are expected in court later on Thursday, April 26, 2007 by Junnier and Smith, who reportedly have reached agreements with prosecutors.

Tesler, with eight months on the job, has vowed to fight charges against him. The three officers were among a team of eight narcotics officers who raided the Johnston's home Nov. 21, 2006 hoping to get a cache of cocaine. They are accused of lying to get a warrant to get into the home. All eight were placed on administrative leave pending the investigation.

14

Deadly Mistakes

The common excuse used by police commissioners and mayors around the country after a Black or Latino life has been unjustly taken is “a mistake was made.” The volume of these mistakes equals to thousands of innocent African-American and Latino lives every year. There is an obvious systemic problem when most of these innocent victims tend to be of African or Latino descent. The casual attitude towards this problem is the alarming factor in all of this. It’s almost as if a Black or Latino life is not valued at all. That attitude is carried throughout the police departments everywhere. The “shoot first and ask questions later” mentality is being reinforced by the higher ranked officials in the police departments. It’s hard not to think that had these victims been white there would be a complete overhaul of the police departments’ tactics.

These deadly, costly mistakes happen on a daily basis and the only surviving victims are usually the families who are left without their loved ones. In most cases, it’s usually someone’s brother, father, mother, daughter or son. Sometimes, it’s also a cousin, a best friend, a companion, a husband, a wife, a boyfriend or a girlfriend. Nevertheless, it’s someone! Some of these victims were the breadwinners for their families and the pillar of strength for their loved ones. As if we don't already have a problem with paternal presence in the black family, but now black men are being taken away by the police at an alarming rate.

These careless cops are afforded the ability to make deadly mistakes because of the loopholes in the law that keeps them from being prosecuted. Police Union big wigs are usually the enforcers behind the discovery for their own truths. We have seen time and time again where police union officials want to show their dedication and alliance to police officers, go through great lengths to make up stories to defend rogue cops' inappropriate actions. These officials are the reason why dirty and incompetent cops aren't fired. These officials are most likely to be white and the only thing that matters to them is keeping an officer on the force at all cost.

If a teacher kills an armed student in his/her classroom, that teacher would most likely end up in prison for murder because people are not supposed to commit murder. Cops are hired to serve and protect, but more and more "kill at will" is becoming a part of their job description.

A mistake is when an officer accidentally discharges his revolver while in a scuffle with a potential criminal. When an officer discharges his service revolver thirty-five times against an unarmed man, it should be classified as murder. It's no accident and it's not a mistake. That officer was out for blood and he wanted to kill by any means necessary. Deadly intent and malicious behavior towards a private citizen is exemplified when an officer "unloads" his weapon and reloads even when fire is not being returned.

The weird thing about this whole situation is that if an attacking dangerous pit-bull terrier was laid to rest with fifty bullets by police officers, people would be angry and demand the prosecution of those officers for animal cruelty. What about human cruelty? People are willing to march for animals, but they frown on the fact that a human life is unjustly taken sometimes. The black man's life has been lessened to that of an animal because we live in a racist society that continues to allow a certain group of people to be abused and mistreated by the system.

These deadly mistakes don't just affect Black and Latino folks; everyone pays for these mistakes. Cities and counties have to pay large sum of money to settle these mistakes in court. Tax payers always contribute one way or another for these deadly mistakes, and not only that, these mistakes are bound to be repeated over and over because the perpetrators are hardly brought to justice, which signifies that it is okay to take an innocent black person's life. Each person who gets killed by a police officer increases the amount of tax we pay to the city or state. The victim doesn't have to be a family member in order for people to be affected. Also, what kind of message are we sending as a society to stand by and allow this type of injustice to take place? Are there no more freedom fighters left? Does no one believe in civil rights anymore?

Situation like these is the catalyst for the bred criminals. When a person feels that nobody gives a shit about him, he's more likely to go out and become anti-social and do things society may deem abnormal.

White kids from the suburbs kill everyday due to the lack of attention from their parents and society, why should it be any different in the hood? Coupled with poverty and the lack of opportunities, Blacks and Latinos have more reason to commit acts of violence, even though they don't. The white kids who kill are hardly referred to as criminals in the media. "Lack of social adjustment and parental guidance" are usually the words used on their behalf when referring to their anti-social behaviors. Any time a minority person commits a crime, he's often looked at as a born criminal who inherited his criminal behavior from his descendants. We have to be careful about the way we're referring to people because mixed marriages among the races are increasing everyday, and soon white parents are going to have to stand up for their black children. A black and white couple cannot have white children according to United States law. Things are gonna have to change real soon in order for us to prosper as a society.

15

Young Black and Dangerous

It usually starts in kindergarten and normally follows us all the way to adulthood. A little Black boy gets into an argument with another little kid whether Black or White; the white teacher usually notices the temper of the Black boy and his lack of social skills. His interaction with his peers usually draws a red flag from a teacher, and most of the time, the teacher's not qualified to do psychological assessments of any kind, but can make recommendations to the principal that the Black child be placed in special education. Some of you may say that I'm exaggerating, but if I recall correctly, it was on national television that a couple of sheriffs in Florida handcuffed, not a little boy, but a little Black girl in elementary school because her teacher didn't have the proper training to deal with her. Yes, I know, unfortunately the violence and abuse is not limited to little Black boys anymore; little Black girls are being treated like criminals as young as eight years old as well.

It's very easy for me to write this book because I'm not making any of this up. The police officers around this country provide more than enough ammunition to make this project possible. The law enforcement officers showed their true colors towards that little Black girl, well-informed of the fact that a camera was rolling and catching their every move. They felt that their action was justified and that the little girl's parent should not have been upset with the way their daughter was treated. No disciplinary action was ever taken against the people involved in the incident. The only person who might be psychologically scarred for life was that little Black girl. And we're right back to special education.

If these officers could do what they did to a little girl, imagine what they would have done to an adolescent Black male. He would've been considered twenty times as dangerous and probably would have left that classroom with Billy clubs stamped all over his face. If they could do what they did in front of a camera, just imagine how many Black males that have been victimized by them without the presence of a camera. The way they handled the little girl was with pure hatred. I would have loved to see their reaction if someone was handling their little girl the same way. Cautionary measures have to be taken because not all of us are as patient and some of us will not stand by and watch the police get away with mistreating our children.

That was just one example that was available on television for the general public to see. What about all those other cases that we don't hear about? There are millions of poor black and Latino families as well as white in some cases that are forced to place their children in special education for the simple fact that they are less fortunate in life. Any form of abnormal behavior from a Black kid in most inner city public school systems is grounds for a psychological assessment by some old white psychologist who feels that the reaction of a kid within a confined setting can deem him/her inappropriate for mainstream education. Unfortunately, these poor parents are usually more than eager to accept the fact that their child needs special education because they stand to collect a check from the government because of the child's disability; completely unaware of the future complications and repercussions that this diagnosis will bring to their child's life. The end result is usually a kid who's forced to cope in an environment not befitting him/her. Furthermore, when he/she reacts to it at the age of sixteen or seventeen, he/she's usually labeled a dangerous criminal. Lack of education from the parents, thus, ends up costing the child a normal, productive life.

Let's look at the people who are responsible for the making of this so called presumed criminal. I stand corrected if I'm wrong, but I've been a victim of criminal presumption plenty of times in my life. I never knew what a criminal really looked like until I had the fingers pointed at me on a few occasions without committing any crime. Anyway, I'm sorry for diverting from the point I was making. The notion that criminals are born is pure garbage. Criminals are created and society bears criminals based on the way these people are treated from an early age. I'm no psychologist, but it's plain and simple to see. Young black kids are not given much of a chance in American society. First of all, the playing fields are not leveled because the inner city kids have too many obstacles that work against them. There's a bunch of teachers who teach in the inner city only because they can't find anything else to do professionally. They usually do such a poor job; they can only find solace by blaming their failure on the students. I'm not talking about those people who teach because of their love for the profession, so please do not take offense to my words if you're a dedicated teacher. And if you're a teacher reading this book, you know exactly who and what I'm talking about. At teacher meetings, they're not shy about calling the students dumb and stupid and most of the time the principals agree with them and encourage them by saying that they understand how tough it is to teach the deprived children of the ghetto. Seventy percent of the teachers who teach in the inner city should have their teaching licenses revoked. The dedicated few continue to fight an uphill battle because the majority always wins.

Unfortunately, those bad teachers are protected by their union. Union officials only see green and they couldn't care less about the education of the students. It's happening in Newark, New Jersey as well New York City and many other major cities around the country. These union officials earn ten times the salary of teachers and most of the time none of them have ever set foot in a classroom.

As a former teacher, I used to hear it all the time from other teachers, "these kids are lazy, they don't want to learn. Half of them don't even want to be here." What these teachers didn't realize was that the kids understood clearly that the teachers didn't want to teach them. As soon as an opening at a better school is available, there's usually a long list of candidates applying. Where's the dedication? I'm baffled by the way Hollywood always portrays these white teachers as saviors of the inner city tribe that they teach at these lowly schools on the big screen. I can't recall such an experience as a youngster. My white teachers couldn't wait to be transferred or sign up for early retirement. I couldn't help feeling stupid after graduating from high school because that's the type of environment that was bred.

The teachers are not the only problem. The fact that most inner city schools are under-funded by state or local government also plays a major role in the kids' failures. I sympathize with the dedicated teachers because I know how tough it is to teach a group of thirty plus kids without an assistant. Many of the kids are not neglected on purpose all the time. However, there are always a few kids that need a special, smaller classroom setting to alter their behavior, but lack of funding keeps them from getting that special attention. These kids are also often labeled and most of the time they try to live down whatever label that's attached to them, and the teachers in turn have to face the consequences.

I worked at a middle school in New York City with the so called "special ed" population, and while there I realized why these kids acted so badly. We had a big white principal who acted more like a bully than an educator. He hired these paraprofessionals to help assist the teachers with the students, but he also instructed them to use any means to discipline these children. I soon found out that these children were being beaten by staff and I even witnessed it once. After reporting it to the Board of Education in New York City, I was suspended without pay for months until the case was resolved months later without the help of a union. All the teachers who worked at the school knew the abuse was going on, but none of them came to my defense or to the children's defense during my hearing, because they had families to feed and they depended on their paychecks. This principal and his staff had been getting away with this for many years until I arrived at the school. I never found out what became of the principal because I never returned to the school. Subsequently, the Board of Education agreed to give me my retroactive earnings and found out through their investigation that the kids had, in fact, been abused for years. I would not be surprised if that principal was given a choice to go to a different school to start the abuse all over again.

Moving teachers around to other schools is a common practice in New York City and around the rest of the country, especially in the inner city. It's not just the cops that get shifted around when they do something illegal or wrong, the teachers get the same treatment and the unions are always happy to fight on behalf of the teachers even when they're wrong. The amount of money that the unions generate is enough to fight Trump in a court room and win. Now, imagine that the police departments in New York City and other major cities have twice that amount to fight their legal battles. They'll always be right in a court of law because the union big wigs just love to show these cops how hard they would fight for them even when they commit pure, unadulterated murder. State prosecutors find it difficult to take police officers' cases to trial because they normally work in cahoots with each other. This book is not about what the teachers are doing wrong or how the system works against minority students, but it's relevant to the development of this so-called group of "dangerous people," which I happen to belong to.

I agree that Black parents need to take a more proactive approach regarding their kids' education as stated by Bill Cosby, but most of those parents have really limited choices. As a youngster, I was left home in my teens to care for my siblings while my parents worked to help provide a stable home for us. It was hard to have the kind of supervision necessary for the type of development that I needed in order to be successful. What they were able to do was instill pride and determination to keep me focused on what I needed to do. However, not all parents are blessed with the foundation my parents had. Further, with the emergence of re-gentrification many parents in the inner city find it even more difficult to even keep food on the table. Housing prices have tripled in most major cities around the country. Most people can't even afford to keep a decent roof over their heads, so it is tough on many families to maintain proper guidance on their children.

What is needed is an increase in federal funding for after-school programs to help these families maintain some kind of control over their children. Most inner city children have no programs to attend after school and thus find themselves hanging out on the streets with their friends, which usually lead to harassment by cops and total chaos in their lives.

Everywhere we turn there's someone telling us how dangerous our children are or they don't want to go to school or learn anything. All those negative comments are sure to have some type of affect on some of these children. Nothing is being done to alleviate the situation. Instead of creating after school programs, law makers are trying to enact anti-loitering laws to make it easier to arrest these children. We'll always have a dilemma in our hands as long as we continue to deprive these young people a good education, access to after school programs and good teachers in the classroom.

16

A Common Sense Solution

The cops who brutally murdered Sean Bell and attempted to murder his two friends are either complete idiots or they were out for blood that night. Had these cps used their commonsense bloodshed could've been avoided that night. It's reported that all police departments require their police officers to undergo psychological testing, but they seem to be missing a few components of that test. Commonsense should be included as part of their psychological evaluation as well as fear.

In the case of Sean Bell, the police officers could've easily intercepted when they claim they heard that one of the victims allegedly said "I'm gonna get my gun." Commonsense should've told them to pull out their badges and identify themselves as police officers and walk these guys to their cars to search the car for a gun. After all, t was because of the mention of a gun that they claim they shot up the car the victims were driving, which ended in cold blooded murder. Police are quick to give probable cause for their illegal searches when there's no need for it, but in the case of Sean Bell where probable cause to search Sean Bell's car was supposedly at their disposal, they turned their backs on it.

It's rather odd that the convenience of probable cause can be used by police only when they choose to exercise that option. It doesn't take a prosecutor or a genius to know that preventing someone from getting to a gun can potentially prevent harm and danger from taking place. Perhaps, being under the influence of alcohol impaired their judgment. If that's the case, sober officers should have been called to the scene to handle the situations. The police department has presented many arguments for their officers' ill actions, but they all seem to lack commonsense. It's understood that undercover officers have to blend-in so their cover is not blown, but at the same time, we know that they are undercover for a reason. Sean Bell and his friends were not part of that reason. They obviously didn't care about blowing their cover or the case they were working because they created a situation where fifty bullets had to be shot for no reason at all, hearsay.

If Sean Bell were shot by civilians, the shooters would have been charged with premeditated murder because their action was based on the preconceived notion that there was imminent danger and instead of trying to diffuse it, they escalated the situation. Since commonsense was irrelevant that night, only murderous intent was present and that's what happened. Murder took place. It's easy to see that these cops are probably going to use the fact that they didn't want to blow their cover at the club as a defense, but a few feet away from it they were willing to engage in a shoot out that exposed their cover to the world, took someone's life in the process and left two other victims, one riddled with eleven bullets and wheelchair bound and the other hoping to recover from the two shots that hit him.

Anybody with commonsense should be able to understand Sean Bell and his friends' reactions to the police when they approached them. It only takes a few seconds for a cop to identify himself to a civilian. Most of the time the badge is dangling around their necks for easy access when they need it, but on the night of the death of Sean Bell all of the officers conveniently failed to pull out their badges to identify themselves as cops. Sean Bell was right to try to run over the unmarked minivan that the cops were driving. In his mind, I'm sure he thought he was being attacked by the guys he had the confrontation with inside the club. It doesn't take a genius to know that if someone pulls out a gun aiming it at you that you should try to run for cover or in Sean Bell's case, try to run them over if you're behind the wheel of a car. He wanted to increase his chances of survival against what he perceived was a group of armed bandits out to kill him. They were bandits, all right, bandits with badges who chose not to display them.

If a police officer is going to be placed in the hood to work undercover, he has to be willing to learn the rules of that neighborhood. Confrontations in the hood sometimes linger beyond control, and at anytime a person may negatively react to a situation. Different survival tactics and mechanisms are used in a confrontation in the hood. Sometimes situations escalate when there's no need for it and we are foolish enough to allow them to get out of control. However, on the night of his death, Sean Bell was trying to live for one more day. He wasn't thinking about the cops, all he and his friends probably thought about were the strangers with guns drawn who were ready to take away their last breath and that they did.

Exposing the badges without the guns would have been sufficed for surrender, I believe. Too much credit is being given to the cop and none to the victims. When commonsense is applied, even a blind man can see that it was a clear cut situation that went wrong on the part of the police because they were out for blood. Police work can be boring and every now and then they like to add a little excitement to their job so that they have something to talk about with their buddies back at the office. The mundane routine and search for excitement concluded with the death of an innocent man.

17

The Officers' Perspectives

In order to be impartial and fair, I decided to talk to a few police officers about some of the events that sometimes lead to the death of many unarmed black victims. These officers came from different backgrounds, upbringing and race. I was surprised and particularly disturbed by some of the responses that I received from these honest officers. I met this one guy in New Jersey while I was browsing a local clothing store in Newark on Springfield Avenue. It's one of those stores that have become a staple in the community and the owner is loved by all. As I waited for my Chinese food order to be filled by one of the many Chinese food joints located in the heart of the ghetto, I decided to walk in to see some of the latest specialty fashion offered by this store/boutique. I found a few items that were interesting, but the prices were very different than I expected, and I also had the bargaining power because the owner wanted to make a sale that evening. While browsing and having a casual conversation with the store owner who happened to be a young Black man doing something very positive in his community, this young officer walked in.

At first, he seemed a little brash and cocky in his demeanor and attitude. He wasn't the smallest guy that

I'd ever seen in a police uniform, but he also wasn't that big either. He was probably no taller than five foot seven inches and weighed between one hundred seventy to one hundred and eighty five pounds. His stomach protruded a little and his physical shape was in question. He was familiar with the owner as he told him that he was coming to pick up something special and to look out for him on a few new items scheduled to arrive at the store in the near future. While the owner and I discussed the alarming murder rate in Newark, New Jersey since the election of newly elected mayor, Corey Booker, the officer listened on and took interest in our conversation. "These jokers are out of control," he said referring to the young black men in Newark who are killing each other everyday for no reason. "Yeah, Newark is hot right now and Booker better do something quick or there won't be any re-election," I said. "It's dangerous out here in these streets," the young cop said angrily. I could feel his frustration because his life is at risk every time he puts on that uniform and walks out the door to go to work. His family has no certainty about his return.

Through the course of our conversation, I found out that the young cop was a second generation police officer. His father was also a cop and had been shot at by an assailant a few years prior. His father was lucky enough to get shot in the leg and survived. So, everyday this young cop worked the streets worrying about his own safety. It was easy for me to segue into the Sean Bell's shooting in New York City because it was a conversation among three intelligent brothers discussing the struggle of survival in the hood. Since Newark, New Jersey is only about a half hour ride from New York City, the Sean Bell shooting was a popular topic there as well. I wanted to hear from a black police officer's perspective why Sean Bell had to die at the hand of police officers when he was unarmed, and why the officers had to fire fifty times. His facial expression and demeanor suddenly changed and his face became serious and I could tell that he was going to be candid with me regardless of how I felt about the situation.

"So you think the fifty shots fired at Sean Bell and his friends were justified?" I asked him bluntly. It was premature for me to bring up Sean Bell's death. The officer stumbled a little before he answered, but with his officer thinking cap on, he didn't waver his allegiance to his fellow officers as he gave me an answer that surprised the hell out me. "I'm not saying what the officers did was right, but I probably would've done the same thing," he said. At this point, I felt like I was talking to the enemy. I was never fond of most cops because of my personal experience with them. I didn't like most white cops because of their racist attitudes towards me and I couldn't stand most black cops because I felt they walked around with a chip on their shoulders. That badge and gun give a black man from the hood something that he's not used to, which is power. Some of them use the power for good, and some of them abuse it. I wasn't sure where this guy stood with me after his statement. "How can you find any justification in this situation?" I asked angrily. "You're a civilian, you'll never deal with the things that I have to deal with on a daily basis on the job," he answered with a cocky cop attitude. Even though it was a friendly conversation, he wanted to make sure I knew he was still authority. After all, he was in uniform and he didn't have to talk to me.

As the conversation went on, I found myself reading the body language of this cop and wondering if my life could be in danger because of cops like him. His explanation of the situation didn't sit well with me at all. In his Newark slang, he started explaining to me why the cops possibly shot fifty times, "If a joker says he's gonna get his gun and when I get outside he tries to run me down, he would've gotten more than fifty shots from me." I tried to bring logic into the situation as a civilian who grew up sometimes in the hood. From the way the cop was speaking, I assumed he grew up in the hood as well. We can almost always identify with our fraternal brothers in the hood through the use of a particular dialect. "Okay, logically, doesn't it make sense that these guys thought that the unmarked van approaching them could have very well been those guys that got into it with them inside the club? And isn't it fair for them to try to run them over if they see their guns drawn? After all, these cops never identified themselves. They simply reacted to something that they heard inside the club," I said. "If a joker says he has a gun, I have to make sure I take him out before he takes me out," the young cop answered. "Well, if that's the case, if those cops had in fact heard that the guy say that he was gonna get his gun, wouldn't it have been more appropriate to subdue him before he got to the car?" I asked. "We don't know the reason why they waited til the guys got to the car. I'm not them and I can't speak for them, but I know that my safety comes before anybody else's and if I had to shoot those guys, I would've done the same thing," he told me.

By then, the logical human side of the young cop had disappeared and I was dealing with the police mentality he adopted from the academy. The expletives were flying out of his mouth a mile a minute as he became overly emotional defending his fellow officers in New York City. "Why fifty shots?" I asked. "There's a lot reasons why fifty shots was fired. None of those cops knew where the first shot came from because the car was surrounded, and none of them had any idea that it was from one of their own. So, automatically they assumed they were being fired upon and in terms started to return fire" he answered. "So, what you're telling me is that without assessing the situation properly, the cops started shooting and it was right that they did that?" I asked. "Shots were being fired from five different people and from five different angles. No one knew for sure that the passengers in that car didn't have a gun, so the cops had to take control of the situation and unfortunately an innocent man got killed," he said. "You're telling me that it's okay for an innocent man to get shot at fifty times and killed by a police officer as long as that officer makes it back home to his family in one piece, right?" I said sarcastically. "Bruh, all I know is my goal is to make it back home to my family in one piece and if I gotta take a joker out to do that, that's what I'd do," he said.

After that last statement, my ignorance radar started going off. The store owner and I couldn't believe this guy's attitude towards an innocent man's death. After realizing that we were noticeably angry with his answers, he attempted to smooth things over. "I probably would've handled the situation a little differently, but I can't say the cops were at fault for doing what they did," he said. He never even realized that his position on the situation still hadn't changed. I could've stood there and talked to this guy for almost two to five hours and he still would've seen the shooting the way he was trained to see it. I even brought up the fact that he's a potential victim because he's a black man and sometimes he has to carry his gun when he's off-duty, and he still defended his comrades.

The only thing I could do was shake my head at him because he was only the tenth officer that I had talked to who shared those same views. I was determined to find a police officer with some commonsense away from the job. I searched and searched and looked and looked, but couldn't find a police officer that could give me a logical explanation for shooting three unarmed men when their life is not at all in jeopardy. By then, I had spoken to about one hundred officers and it was unanimous that they all would've reacted the same way if they were faced with the same situation. However, none of the officers were honest enough with me to tell the reasoning behind the way they would've reacted. I couldn't find a cop in Boston, New York City, New Jersey, Philadelphia or Atlanta to tell me the reasoning behind their thinking. That is until I went to Washington DC and met a twenty-four-year veteran who worked homicide most of his career with the police department.

This officer deserves a name because he was the most candid of all of them. We'll call him John to protect his identity. John is not your typical officer, but he's very passionate about his job. He lives and breathes his job and can't seem to get himself away from it. According to John, he's living his childhood dream, working the job that he was born to do. Those were his true words and I swear I wouldn't make them up. John is a dedicated cop in every sense of the word. An officer who's been shot at and also has shot people that he regretted shooting. You'd have to know him personally to understand that malice never plays a role in his actions. I can only guess that he's about six feet one-two inches tall and weighed about two hundred and twenty to two hundred and thirty pounds. Although he has an athletic build, he doesn't look intimidating at all. John looks like your average teddy bear. His tone is pleasant and his demeanor friendly. When I first met him I could not tell that he was a cop. He was very laid back and nonabrasive unlike some of the cops I met while working on this book. What I like most about John is that he doesn't allow the fact that he works as a cop to alter his personality. John doesn't take on the persona of a cop. He understands that it is a job. He's always quick to say that he works as a cop.

We met through a mutual friend during a business trip in Washington D.C. He and I and our mutual friend hung out and we had a great time the first time we met at this club. A few months went by before I saw John again and this time I was a little more excited to see him because I knew I had this project that I was working on and I wanted to hear his opinion and point of view about the Sean Bell shooting in New York. I figured he heard about the police officers who shot and killed this young man named Sean Bell on the night before his wedding while leaving a club in the Queens section of New York. At first, he was vague about the details of the shooting, but after he allowed me to explain what happened according to documented reports in New York, he understood that the actions the cops took were extreme. However, John's candid attitude differs greatly from the other cops that I spoke with.

While John may have agreed that the cops' actions were extreme, he didn't feel that they were inappropriate. I was baffled because I never expected a brother who grew up in the hood and understands greatly the harassment that most of us suffer on the daily basis at the hands of the cops would sympathize with the cops. First, he wanted to put everything in perspective for me and that meant that I had to hear about his training, the fear that comes along with the job and what the cops deal with overall on a daily basis. I wasn't as patient as he wanted me to be while he talked. I interrupted him a few times because I was riled up after he told me that the cops' actions weren't inappropriate. I wanted to get to the point where he thought perhaps there was anything appropriate about the incident. Although he was different from most cops, he also shared some of their traits. Usually, most officers want to be heard and with authority and they don't like to listen and he was no different. His information was far more important than mine because he was a police officer. His interpretation of events carried more weight than mine because he was the one that had to deal with deadly consequences on a daily basis. As far as he was concerned, I've never been anything more than a civilian.

I can be as combative and stubborn as a lion when the fiery passion inside of me is ignited by a sensitive issue. I was trying to find answers that only a Black man can understand and accept. In this new setting during our second meeting, John carried the burden of being a cop on his shoulders just like the rest of the police officers I'd met. Then finally, after disagreeing about police procedures back and forth for about an hour, I struck a chord. "How come we never hear about any unarmed white boys getting shot by police officers anywhere in this country?" I asked. "White boys are most likely to follow orders, "he answered. "So, you're saying that all black men are defiant and they never follow the orders of the police?" I asked with a devilish grin. I had opened a whole new can of worm. I never anticipated the next words coming out of his mouth.

"These Negroes act a fool and you know that. I'm more likely to be shot by one of them then a white boy. There's always a possibility of being shot by one of these knuckleheads in the hood. I know it's not fair, but we are prejudice against black men because of their crime history," he said. It's not like he was telling me anything new, but their perception of black men put all of us at risk regardless of the fact that some of us have criminal intent or not.

John went on to tell me how cops are not as afraid of potential white offenders as they are with blacks. They are taught this at the police academy. The shooting of black men have more to do with skin color than racism itself. The statement is oxymoronic, but from black point of view, as John explained it to me, blacks are also more dangerous as well. So it's not necessarily racism that is used in extreme circumstances where these young men are shot, but the fear of their skin color. According to John, the police academy makes more references to stereotypes during training than the segregated south did in the fifties.

John was not the only officer who admitted this little fact to me. I would later talk to one of my good friend who's also a cop in a different city in the northeast and he would confirm all that John had to say to me. White cops in position of authority display their racist attitudes openly at the precincts. Even their fellow black officers are sometimes subjected to their racism, and these events usually go without a hitch or a complaint in the officers' files.

One of the nicest individuals I ever met happened to be a law enforcement officer from Gwinnett County in Georgia. To be a little more specific, he's a Deputy Sheriff. He's a man of great integrity and the patriarch in his family even though he's one of the youngest siblings. My encounter with him took place while he was helping take care of a legal matter involving one of my tenants in Georgia. He explained to me how he experienced the brunt of racism in New York City while on he was on a special trip to attend the funeral of an NYPD Officer. While he was in the company of a few white officers, he noticed that one particular officer kept using racial epithets and attacking black people as if the nice sheriff was an offender with total disrespect and disregard for the man as a Deputy Sheriff.

After this staunch racist NYPD Officer made too much reference to the man as a boy, the Deputy Sheriff decided to put him in his place by simply repeating a metaphoric statement that he had once heard from somewhere. He simply said, "You ever have a pair of shoes that you bought because you wanted them, but you never wear them, then one day you decide to polish them. The broken leather is brought back to life with a polish to it and suddenly the shoe is not so old anymore." This motorcycle officer was baffled and caught off-guard at the same time. He had underestimated the black officer from Georgia, but even worst, he exposed something that we all know to well exists within the NYPD, racism. This Deputy Sheriff left an impression on me and I plan on calling him from time to time to see how he and his family are doing.

Another problem that was revealed during my interviews with some of the officers is that the cowardice cops on the force are known. Most of the time, they only talk about their fear of situations and how close and often they normally come to shooting at people. Their service revolver becomes a guide in everything they do, even when it's not necessary. These are the officers most of the time who shoot first, then ask questions later.

18

A Police Mentality

After talking to so many officers including some of my childhood friends who are cops, I came to the conclusion that there is such a thing as a "cop mentality." A cop mentality is very different than that of a civilian. Every cop leaves his/her house everyday praying and hoping that they make it back home after their shift is over. While most of them are aware of the dangers associated with their profession, many of them walk around with this fear that their life can be taken at any time without a moment's notice. And it is that fear that places the lives of the rest of us in jeopardy. The common statement I heard from these cops was "I need to make sure I make it back home to my family at any cost." That's a deadly statement if you ask me. It's not like these people are soldiers in Iraq having to look over their shoulders every minute for a pursuing insurgent. However, that's the mentality that they carry with them. So in the hood, it's Guerilla warfare all the time.

That mentality carries with it deadly consequences. When a cop walks around in fear everybody is a possible suspect and a dangerous criminal. Every little situation can be blown out of proportion because of that fear. I witnessed one incident where two cops were called to the scene of a domestic dispute. One was an African-American female officer and the other was a Caucasian male officer. The wife was enraged because she suspected that her husband was cheating on her, as a result, she assaulted him and punched him on the mouth, which was evident. The man reacted and pushed the woman to the floor after which she called the cops. They must've patched things up during the time it took the cops to finally respond to the scene. However, the male officer ordered the husband to the floor with his gun drawn when he showed up and blew the whole scene out of proportion after he was given access to the apartment. The female officer seemed a little too familiar with the scene and noticed that her partner was overreacting like super cop. She tried to take charge of the situation to diffuse it before things got out of hands. Before she got a chance to talk to the couple, the white officer was insulting the husband telling him, "That's all you people do is beat up on your women." His comment infuriated the husband and he got a reaction out of him. To make a long story short, the officer at some point felt his life was being threatened and the situation ended up with the strike of a baton upside the man's head and a bloody mess for no reason. The female officer obviously didn't agree with his approach to the situation, but she had to support him to show a united front. As a witness assessing the situation, the cop should have carried the blame for the events that led to the man's hospitalization. However, the police were not interested in taking a statement from me. Civilians are not allowed to monitor police behavior even though our taxes pay their salaries, unless of course, the monitoring benefits them.

It's the cop mentality that nearly cost that man his life and probably cost him a few years of his life in prison for something that could've easily been diffused. The male officer thought he could insult the man without any repercussion because he represented the law. That officer created an environment where he became afraid of the man's reaction and when he acted on his fear, someone else paid the price with a beating and time in prison.

It's routine how these situations take place everyday in the hood. The cops will escalate situations or even instigate people into reacting to them. Once that happens, their fears take over, usually resulting in excessive or deadly force against innocent victims. The fear that these cops harbor is profound. Across the board, most of the police officers I've talked to confirmed that they would've reacted to the Sean Bell situation almost in similar fashion, but not because they hate Black men, but because of the fear of them.

The "shoot first" mentality of cops seems to be adopted at the academy. There are profilers at the academy who lists certain groups as being more dangerous than others and certain behaviors are more prevalent from some people. That kind of teaching places a whole race of people in jeopardy everyday. If a profiler is teaching a cadet that I'm more likely to be armed or commit a crime because I wear comfortable baggy jeans, Timberland boots and a sweatshirt, that means my livelihood can be taken from me at any time. It's another form of racial profiling. It may not be taken place behind the wheel of a car, but it's profiling nonetheless.

Contagious shooting is another form of justification often used to defend cops who suffer from this disease known as "cop mentality." It's hard as a civilian for me to grasp the transformation that takes place when someone puts on a uniform to go to work as a cop, but where does the human side go? Is there any compassion being taught at the academy? Since when does it take a group of cops to shoot fifty bullets into a car to overcome the fear of going home safely to one's family? Contagious shooting is explained as almost a knee jerk reaction when cops are involved in a police shoot-out. Often times they say that the shooter naturally reacts with the discharge of his pistol when gunshots are heard. And gunshots are heard quite often in some parts of the ghetto, so everybody in the ghetto is at risk.

Despite the fear that these cops claim to have, through my research, I still found that a white cop is more likely to shoot a black victim in most cases. Black police officers are more able to control this fear because some of them grew up in that environment. Female officers are less likely to draw their guns to shoot at innocent people. Something has to be said of that cop mentality because the female cops are less likely to overreact in any situation. Are these white male officers too afraid to be in the black community? If so, shouldn't the academy improve their training to help these cops overcome the fear that they have for the hood?

The "cop mentality" doesn't allow room for error when it has to do with the life of cops. The "cop mentality" also allows them to dig into a victim's past to justify their inappropriate actions. A traffic ticket can suddenly be a black spot on a dead victim's record when the cop mentality is used. That cop must be defended and protected at all cost, even if a victim's character has to be defamed.

The cop mentality also allows police officers to process information differently when it comes to Black people. One cop in particular told me that when white folks are pulled over by police officers, they know to keep their hands on the steering wheel. I'd like to see the pamphlet that was handed out to white people that informs them so well of what to do when they're pulled over by a cop. I've been in a car with white people when they were very disobedient to cops and nothing happened to them. Even on television, I see that white people are more likely to get angry at cops than Black people. Most Black people know to keep their mouth shut when they're pulled over by a cop because most of the time the cop is just looking for a fraction of a reason to let loose a few bullets or use his baton to subdue a Negro.

Someone with a mental disorder who acts a little abnormal is perceived as a threat to them. The cops are very much into body language, but they lack the capacity to make sound decisions when it matters most in situations involving Black and Latino folks. The criminal cop's mind works like any common criminal. Often times they can't keep an illegal act to themselves, they feel the need to brag about their adventure. However, the cop mentality creates a safe haven for them because cops are not supposed to rat out other cops.

I've even had a personal experience in New York City where my car was being ticketed for no reason at all, when I went to court, I was forced to pay the tickets despite the fact that the cop had fabricated the tickets. Undercover news investigations have exposed these rogue cops all over New York City. However, what I found most appalling was the fact that I was told that it was common practice by a family member who's a police officer when I brought up the subject during a family gathering. A family member who has been a New York City police officer for over a decade informed me that he has written tickets on cars where people talked back to him or when he didn't like a particular person. "It's your word against the cop in court. Who do you think the judge is going to believe?" he said. That goes to show that all the branches work together. The cops bring the criminals to court, the prosecutors prosecute them, and the judges sentence them based on the statement of the cops. It's not a fair game at every turn. No police station in New York City would give me the number for Internal Affairs when I asked to report this cop for writing fake tickets on my car.

I truly don't believe that all police officers want to adhere to the cop mentality. However, most of them have no choice. They either in or they're out, and nobody wants to be out because the danger of no back-up response to a grave situation when an officer who's out is greater than anything that the officer can possibly face on the job. Police officers have to rely on each other for support and back up, and when they feel that a person can't be trusted as an officer, they'll find plenty of reasons to justify why a call didn't come in. These sentiments are shared by many black police officers.

19

A Pattern of Harassment

All it takes for someone to realize how easy it is for a young Black male to get a police record is for a police officer to see that young Black man standing on any corner in any inner city street or suburb for more than ten minutes. First, it's that bored patrolman who feels that it is his duty to find out why the young man has been standing idle for more than ten minutes. America, land of the free my ass! Why is it that a young Black male can't chill on his block anymore? If the police are paid and trained to investigate drug dealers, they should be able to recognize and identify who the drug dealers are. Of course, the authority in their voice when they're inquiring about a Black male's personal business is enough to get a middle finger from any young man. Ignorant of their first amendment rights, these young guys usually don't realize that they don't have to answer any questions, not that the cops don't respect those rights either. One question leads to another and before he knows it, a young Black male is being handcuffed for either loitering or disorderly conduct. Many of them, including me, never think much of a disorderly conduct charge, but it's just part of the process, and there's usually more to come.

Now, every time the police addresses this young man he feels the need to give them an answer and most of the time they're accusing him of something he's not even doing and if he gets angry, he's labeled "belligerent" and the next thing he knows he's back down at the station getting booked on some trumped up charges. This time the judge orders probation and slowly but surely the charges increase each time. Sooner or later this young man ends up serving a sentence just because he wanted to hang out on his block and became defiant when a cop with a chip on his shoulder wanted to prove his authority. How do I know about all of this? I've witnessed it and I've been a victim of it. Police harassment is a common thing in the hood.

I have been arrested many times for no reason at all by police. Not in New York City, but in Boston where I grew up. No one ever forgets the first time they're handcuffed. I remember it like it happened yesterday. We used to go to this under 21 Nightclub in Weymouth, Massachusetts every Sunday. When the club let out the cops would harass us. One particular Sunday night while we were coming out the club, a friend's sister was in front of me and this cop with a complex, cut in front of me to get behind her. Out of the blue, he pulled out his baton and started pushing and shoving her from the back like an animal. At fifteen years old, I recognized injustice when I saw it. "Why are you pushing her?" I asked. "Shut the hell up before I lock you up," he answered. "Lock me up! For what? Cause you're trying to beat on a girl?" Before I knew it I had four cops on me swinging their batons and I'm using my hand to block them to keep from getting hit. Within seconds, I was subdued and taken to a police station and charged with disorderly conduct.

Fortunately for me at the time, I was under age and the case was continued without a finding for six months. Another technique used by the judges to insure a criminal record in case of a slip up. "Continue without a finding" means that the white judge didn't believe that I was innocent and he was willing to give me another six months to demonstrate that I was not a trouble maker. Or better yet, another six months to find reasons to lock me up. How lucky was I? I got shoved and beaten by the cops, but I had to prove that I was innocent to some judge who didn't even want to hear my version of the events. If I had been seventeen years old at the time, I would have had a criminal record all because a cop wanted to abuse his power.

Far worse has happened to me since then and nowadays when the cops ask for my ID, they almost always have their gun drawn because I'm a processed criminal without a criminal record. What I mean by "processed" is that each time I was arrested on some trumped up charges, it showed up on the computer when they do a background check. I have never been convicted of any crime, but the paper trail on me is very thick. That's how it all begins. One arrest here for no reason and another there and before you know it, a charge is stuck when you least expect it and all of a sudden you're a known criminal according to the police department. I have managed to avoid a criminal record despite the efforts of the police.

Another thing I learned is that there's no such thing as a case not remaining on record. The first thing a prosecutor wants to point out to a judge when a person goes to court is the number of times they've been arrested, whether there was a conviction or not. It's good to have a case thrown out, but the court will always remind you that they're building a case against you and anything you did in the past increases your chances of guilt the next time you're in court for another matter. Giuliani and his cohorts in New York City have proven that point over and over whenever one of his criminal cops killed someone. There's no limit to what they would do; even sealed juvenile records aren't safe.

To this day, I'm still trying to understand the meaning of "disorderly conduct." The cops have too much leeway with this charge. Anybody can be charged with disorderly conduct at the cop's discretion. It also becomes an abuse of power because when everything else fails, they can charge you with disorderly conduct.

I know I'm not the only person who gets angry when a cop from out of nowhere comes to my neighborhood and tells me what I can and cannot do, especially if I'm not breaking any laws. I see white people walk out of their house and loiter around their neighborhood for as long as they want and they're not harassed, why can't black people do the same thing in their neighborhood? I never lived in any projects; I grew up in a middleclass neighborhood where everyone worked for a living. How wrong were my parents when they thought "middleclass" would somehow shield me from police harassment? We're a threatening group of people for no reason at all. The mere presence of a black man intimidates mostly everyone in this society; and don't let it be more than two Black men because now it's a gang situation.

Thirty drunken white boys can roam the streets at all hours of the night and nothing will happen to them.

They're often referred to as "frat boys," an endearing term. Thirty sober Black guys walking down the street talking quietly becomes a SWAT team situation or a gang unit situation. The dogs are usually brought out along with the riot gear, tear gas and mace. The common command to "get on the ground" better be obeyed or we'll find our body jerking with three thousand volts of electricity from their taser guns or worst, we might be dancing to the sounds of gunshots at the hands of the officers.

This pattern of harassment of Black men has been established all over the country in every major city. The cops want to be able to tell us when, where and how far and how long we can walk. They also have the authority to restrict the number of Black men that should be together at once in a public place. Some people are completely unaware of this behavioral pattern, but look closely and you'll find that it exists and it's prevalent in the Black neighborhoods.

All police departments are aware of the hot zones for drugs in their municipalities and most of the offenders are known to them, but why do they continue to harass innocent people? The problem *must be* the new drug dealers sprouting in every home in the black community everyday. I've actually heard young kids say, "They already think that I'm a drug dealer, I might as well sell drugs." The "they" that they are referring to in this instance is usually the police. I have heard the horror stories from my former students and I sympathized with them because I've been victimized on many occasions, as a young man.

It goes to show that there's no such thing as a clean record once you've been arrested by any cops from anywhere in the country. When it comes to Black men, police departments across the nation adopt this gang mentality. And sometimes a person has to question whose blueprint the street gangs decided to follow when they first thought about their inception. The police department's blueprint seems to be a perfect fit, especially with a guy like Giuliani as mayor. He should be prosecuted for committing crimes against the Black citizens of New York City. A man with no morals who cheated on his wife and kept a mistress for many years is now trying to lead the most powerful nation in the world. This country will be "Nazi America" if he gets elected.

The police in Boston almost made a serious criminal out of me back in 1990. Even a white suburbanite understood that he could exploit the Black community and its Black men. Charles Stewart knew that all it would take was his word to say that a heinous crime had been committed against his wife in the predominantly Black section of Boston known as Roxbury. Armed with a hand gun and a plan to frame a black man, any black man, for his crime in order to cash out on an insurance policy he had taken on his wife, Charles Stewart decided to shoot his pregnant wife to death and himself in the stomach and then blamed it on a black man. Many Black men were rounded up like by the cops who acted like they were part of a lynch mob looking for the murderer who had taken the life of a white woman and damn near killed her husband. I happened to be in the Grove Hall section where an all points bulletin went out for all Negroes befitting my description. I was thrown against a wall, strip searched and provoked, but I stayed cool because a life sentence was imminent if I said the wrong thing.

After watching the police terrorized the black community and the lives of many young men for weeks, Charles Stewart realized his story couldn't hold up. Unbeknownst to the police department at the time was that the calculated murderer was Charles Stewart himself. Unable to deal with the consequences of his actions when he was found out, he cowardly took his own life by jumping in the Charles River. It was ironic he lost his life in a river that shared his first name.

Even Susan Smith in South Carolina tried to exploit the negative image of the Black man in October 1994 when she killed her own children, then blamed it on a Black man. The only reason why these things continue to happen is because of the history of the Black man being unjustly named as the perpetrators in crimes since we arrived in this country against our will. Nothing has changed because the same tactics are still being used in a new way of business.

Stories like this take place everyday because society continues to perpetuate this negative image of Black men and the black community as a whole. Whenever white people want to portray themselves as victims to the police, they know all too well that all they have to do is point to the black community and fabricate whatever crime suits them. Back then, it was the Klu Klux Klan that gathered a group of racists for a lynch mob. Today it's the boys in blue with their badges and guns drawn that show up for the lynching. We live in a society that has established a pattern of punishment for Black men that is over two hundred years old and these patterns continue to exist because they're now masked with new policies, laws and rules.

A lot of major cities are enacting laws preventing more than five persons to publicly congregate at once. I'm sure those laws aren't being passed because too many white kids are walking the streets together. Cities like Chicago, Boston, New York and many others enacted anti-loitering laws allowing police to disperse any group of two people or more "without just cause or purpose," which violates our civil right to congregate. According to the ACLU in Illinois, about 41,000 of mostly African-Americans and Latinos became victims of that law. They were arrested under its provisions. Even though the law was struck down by the Supreme Court as it was ruled unconstitutional because it violated the right to freedom of movement. The City of Chicago appealed the decision to have it reversed.

It is also common to find youths in particular areas of any major cities being harassed by police simply because of the clothes that they wear. Often, these "offenders" are taken to a precinct and their "mug shots" are placed in books to be shown to potential victims in case of a crime. I can personally attest to this because it happened to me as well. A personal friend was a victim of a crime and when he got to the police station in the Mattapan section of Boston, my mug shot was presented to him even though I have never been convicted of a misdemeanor or felony crime. I tried getting my picture removed, but the police department told me there was nothing I could do about it.

A study found in Michigan showed that white kids are more likely to be let go at the scene of a crime if stopped or arrested by a police officer than black kids. Black kids often have to prove their innocence before they're released while the white kids' words are usually enough to render a release. Look of suspicions is the term often used by police officers when they stop a black youth for no apparent reason. Suspicions can be defined by the court in many ways and officers hide behind it to continue to harass Black youths.

In a city where only twenty four percent of the population is black, it was reported by the New York Police Department's own analysis that 55.2 percent of the people stopped by the cops were African-American. While police stopped 508,540 individuals in 2006, over half of those individuals stopped were black. The likelihood of black men being stopped by cops in New York City for no reason at all is three times that as whites. Over 67,000 black men were stopped by New York City officers per quarter last year. Complaints involving "police stops" have account for 33 percent of all complaints against cops in New York City. Black men are more likely to be harassed by police in New York City, which increases the chance of arrest by 500 percent. Most of the time, cops are able to lie about the reasons to mask their illegal stops of Black men by fabricating "just cause" in their reports.

20

Establishing a Police State

It's easy to see how a pattern of abuse was established in New York City, under then, mayor Giuliani. Every time a black life was taken, the mayor jumped the gun to defend his officers without gathering the facts. It was as if Giuliani never left the courtroom as a prosecutor. He made his feelings known about viewing most black men as criminals while he was in office, but no one ever bothered to check how many innocent victims are behind bars because of Giuliani's own prejudices and racist attitudes towards black men while he was a prosecutor.

Giuliani embellished the dismissed charges against murder victim Patrick Dorismond into the image of an habitual criminal to defend the officer who unjustly shot and took his life, creating a pattern that allowed cops to believe as long as the victims were of a darker complexion, there would be no repercussion from the police department. In Giuliani's eyes, every black or Latino man that was ever shot by one of his officers deserved to be dead. His common practice of referring to murder victims as "common criminals" was often documented on the news during his press conferences after a shooting. Even when there wasn't any proof of any criminal history, Giuliani would find ways to smear the victims' names in the media to justify the actions of his police officers. Thank goodness for term limits in New York City or we would have had a basket case of a lifetime dictator in our hands.

More police brutality and abuse took place under the Giuliani administration in New York City than any other administration. When evidence proved to the fact that Abner Louima had indeed been victimized by police during Giuliani's tenure in office, he dismissed the case as an "exception that proves the rule" involving a few rogue cops because Internal Affairs and a few other officers were forced to give testimonies. It was only after a jury found the cops guilty on countless charges that Giuliani made his statement. Had it not been for a nurse who reported the case to the newspapers that made the headlines for weeks, the officers involved in the Abner Louima case would've been defended just as tirelessly by Giuliani.

Giuliani, who at the time was focused on his campaign for election to the US Senate as the Republican candidate from New York State against Hillary Clinton, was trying to protect or speak to an upwardly mobile audience residing primarily in Manhattan. The corporate elite of Manhattan was the reason why he became mayor in the first place, as well as some of the middle class who had grown wealthy off of the stock market boom and decided that they needed to feel a lot safer because they had more money . At the time, they poured millions of dollars into his campaign. Giuliani was declaring his resolve to defend their interests by allowing cops to run wild like cowboys with their guns drawn on the streets of New York City clearing the paths for these rich millionaires and ridding the streets of its criminal element by any means necessary. Police searches and the occasional shooting of innocent workers and youth, he told them, were an acceptable means of policing as long as the rich felt safe, which created a great social divide between the city's wealthy and the tremendously large population of impoverished and largely minority and immigrant rejects.

Giuliani wasn't alone in his decisions to back New York City officers at all cost. Fully aware of the power of the Police Benevolent Association, the mayor knew that he needed a strong force behind him. During Abner Louima's trial it was revealed that there was a wider phenomenon of murderous brutality and rampant corruption within the NYPD. Breaking the alliance with a "fellow officer" is the worst betrayal of the badge and brotherhood even if police officers had to compromise their own integrity and risk their own livelihood in the process.

According to published reports, the Louima trial also exposed the role of the PBA, which provided a key element of the so-called "Blue Wall of Silence" under which cops systematically lied about incidents of police abuse. The practice was so common that, as was reported by the 1994 Mollen Commission, formed to investigate a raging scandal over brutality and drug-trafficking by police, officers themselves talk about "testilying" in court. It appears as if we have law upholding criminals monitoring unlawful criminals? I guess the badge legitimizes their criminal activities and the gun and the hundreds of thousands members give them the protection they need in order to function as an illegal empire.

Called as a hostile witness by the prosecution was Michael Immitt, a PBA trustee, roughly the equivalent of a business agent, who chaired a meeting in which the prosecution said, the plot was hatched to lie about Officer Schwarz's presence during the bathroom assault. Immitt claimed on the stand that he did not know the nature of the charges the cops were facing, even on the day that the attack on Louima made banner headlines in the daily papers.

Also called to the stand was Anthony Abate, a former PBA 70th Precinct delegate who was fired from the Police Department for using racial slurs against a black cop and lying about an obscenity-laced tongue-lashing he had given a young female officer after she tried to deliver a lecture on domestic violence at the stationhouse. Asked about scores of phone calls made to him by the officers involved in Louima's arrest after revelations of his ordeal first surfaced, he claimed that his only role had been to lend the cops "a sympathetic ear."

Weise and Volpe were the two main suspects in the Louima case. Weise succeeded Abbate as a precinct delegate, while JustinVolpe's brother also held that post in the union. This was hardly the first case of union delegates being implicated in cases of extreme brutality. Everybody worked together to cover corruption and the main defender was always the man elected by the people. We were duped by Giuliani back then in New York City and I hope that America is not duped by him the same way we were duped by George Bush. I'm still trying to figure out what makes Giuliani think that he's qualified to be our president.

21

Giuliani and the Gang

It was revealed during the officers' trial of the attack on Louima that Officer Justin Volpe was not secretive about his villainous attack on Louima. Instead, he boasted about his actions throughout the stationhouse with the bloody, excrement stained stick that he used to sodomize Louima in his hand, and proclaimed how he had "broken a man down." His cowardice act was spread amongst the officers minutes after it happened, but the gang had to stick together because they're supposed to have each other's back regardless of inappropriate behavior by their fellow officers. Not one officer stepped forward to report the heinous crime that took place at the police station. The "blue code of silence" is just as effective as the Street Code of Justice among gangs on the street. Justin Volpe and his fellow gang members at the Brooklyn station were proud that one of their own had broken a man down and it would've gone unreported if it hadn't been for a nurse at the hospital who alerted the authorities on behalf of Abner Louima.

It appears as if solidarity is the only way to survive in the New York Police Department much like a street gang. Most gang members can't leave a gang without suffering the repercussions with their life and it's the same with the NYPD and any other police departments around the country. I've talked to many police officers who have seen injustice take place in front of them and I was told that there's nothing that they can do about it because their fellow officers are more dangerous than the street gang members. These officers rely on their partners and other officers for back up in grave situation and it's very easy for them to be caught in "friendly fire" when they go against the grain. What kind democracy is this? This gang mentality adopted by the police reinforces the deviant behaviors and encourage officers to act disorderly while on the job because they know that they're protected by the "blue code of silence." You don't have to read this book to know that it's been documented over and over by the media that cops who testified against their own have been labeled rats just as if they were part of a street gang. Death threats over the phone and through letters are also common for those who stand up against the injustice caused by their fellow officers.

The "Stop Snitching" campaign on the street, which I will elaborate on in a later chapter, had to have been adopted from the NYPD. Police officers are labeled snitches when they testify against their fellow officers and most of the time they are shunned from the police department. I guess the street gangs have a lot to thank the police for. The blueprint that they follow seems to come directly from the police.

Shortly after police shooting victim, Patrick Dorismond's lifeless body was identified by his grieving wife, the Giuliani administration launched a campaign filled with obscenities to berate the dead man as an habitual criminal who was destined for the penal system or a police bullet. With the police department's back against the wall, Giuliani, the chief gangster, ordered the then Police Commissioner Howard Safir to unseal a juvenile record on Dorismond, disclosing that he had been arrested for robbery and assault when he was thirteen years old. Giuliani acted like the former prosecutor and gangster that he is by starting a smearing campaign in an attempt to defend the actions of the police officers. I am certain there are men who are sitting in jail today because of Giuliani's prejudices, inappropriate actions and racist attitude towards black men. He was once quoted as saying that "most of the offenders committing crimes are black." This is the same man who thinks he's ready to become America's president and leader.

Dorismond's juvenile record reportedly stemmed from a childhood fist fight over a quarter with another kid. The case was dropped and his record sealed because he was a minor. However, Giuliani took the position that once he was dead, Dorismond's right to keep his police records from his childhood sealed by the mayor died with him. The cocky Giuliani was confident that by declaring Dorismond "no altar boy" and that his prior brush with the police may justify to the public the fact that a police officer had taken his life.

The cowardice cop who shot the innocent Dorismond was by praised Giuliani for his "distinguished" career as a police officer, reinforcing the belief that shooting an innocent, unarmed Black man to death in the street was warranted. He was quoted as saying the officer "put his life on the line in the middle of the night to protect the safety and security of this city." I wonder how an unarmed man jeopardized the safety of the citizens of New York City. The only person whose life was on the line was Dorismond.

While Giuliani was quick to point out Dorismond's record, he remained silent about the police officer's own work record, which as a matter of fact recorded that the shooting of an unarmed man was not out of character at all for the officer. The cop's record reflected the fact that he had shot his neighbor's dog with his service revolver for no reason at all even before he graduated from the police academy.

The situation was no different when Sean Bell was shot to death by police officers back in the November of 2006, the night before his wedding. Thank God Giuliani was no longer in office because he would have ordered a lynch mob to go after Sean Bell's character to prove that his police department was right in shooting an unarmed man to death. Nevertheless, even with a new mayor, the same similar tactics were used by the police. Although mayor Bloomberg showed more sympathy for the victim in the beginning, he later changed his position to side with the police as the investigation unfolded. It was alleged that a fourth man was in the car when Sean Bell was killed even after police admitted that they surrounded the car when they opened fire. The projects where Sean Bell grew up were terrorized because police was looking for a scapegoat to justify their actions. A fourth suspect had to be found quickly because the public wouldn't buy any justification for the shooting.

In the midst of a hail of fifty bullets a fourth suspect somehow managed to get away with a gun while his friends were all hit with bullets. The story sounded better than a concoction brewed at the Anheuser Busch mills by Mr. Busch himself since the cops claimed they surrounded the car and the reason why fifty bullets were shot was because of the crossfire among cops. Surely enough, one of these cops would have given chase when they saw the fourth suspect running with a gun in his hands. It was easier to say after the fact that there was a fourth suspect despite what eyewitnesses have told investigators. Police officers lie worst than gang members and we have people in the system who continue to support their lies. How can there ever be justice when cops are allowed to lie to justify senseless murders that they are committing against unarmed citizens?

The NYPD gang was also in full effect when 23-year old Malcolm Ferguson was shot to death by police officers. Then gang leader Rudy Giuliani, declared in his trademark sneer that "the 23-year-old Ferguson was no Diallo and that police officer Louis Rivera, who pumped a fatal bullet into the back of the unarmed man's head during a struggle allegedly witnessed by two people, is the true hero." He was conveniently comparing two victims to make a hero out of his murderous officer.

According to published news accounts of the events, prior to Ferguson's death, he had taken part in a protest against police brutality for the murder of Amadou

Diallo by NYPD Officers. "We were just speaking our minds like everybody else and we were just grabbed because they wanted to break the protest up," charges Josh S., a then 17-year-old member of the pressure group Refuse & Resist. "It was a strategy that the cops had set up. Actually, my arresting officer told me he was going to charge me with resisting arrest, but he was going to be nice and not do this. I told him he wasn't supposed to arrest me in the first place. He said he knew that, but that's just the way it works." Again, a gang member demonstrated how he had to follow the leader's orders by placing a young man under arrest for no reason at all.

Josh S. spent a night in the cell with Ferguson. "When we were there we were angry," he recalls. "We spent more time in jail than the cops who shot Diallo. They didn't even spend any time in jail, so you can imagine how we were feeling." Ferguson participated in the jailhouse discussion about eroding civil rights under the Giuliani administration. "Everybody in the cell was sharing the same sentiment of anger and rage over this whole situation," says Josh S.

As retaliation for his involvement in the march to protest the death of Amadou Diallo, Malcolm Ferguson became a target of NYPD officers. The morning after the Ferguson shooting, Giuliani fired back at those who were comparing Ferguson to Diallo. Giuliani called the killing of Ferguson a completely different situation. He described Ferguson as a "career criminal" who had a long record of robbery, burglary, heroin trafficking, gun possession, and resisting-arrest charges, while Diallo had no rap sheet. "He'd been arrested several times while on parole, but somehow was never put back in prison, which is where people who violate parole should go," the mayor scoffed. Diallo had no rap sheet, but he somehow unjustly ended up with forty one bullets in him at the hand of Giuliani's gang members. The nerve of Giuliani to use the man's spotless record in vain to defend his police officer… We can already see how his campaign is going to be shaped. Giuliani will use anything to his advantage and I'm sure that America won't be duped again.

Another highlighted reason for the possible killing of Malcolm Ferguson was the fact that he had also filed a civil suit against New York City and its Police Department (NYPD) over an earlier arrest in which his hand was broken by cops and was left without medical attention as was the case with Abner Louima. Some neighbors and friends suggested that he may have been executed for seeking legal redress to police brutality.

"He was just a human being," says Josh S. "They didn't know he was an ex-con when they killed him." The night after Ferguson was killed, Josh S. went back to Soundview, protesting. "Everybody was obviously very angry," he says. "We were all feeling the same, fearing for our own safety from the people who are supposed to protect us and serve us. . . " According to published reports. Of course, no one expected Rudy Giuliani to embrace Malcolm Ferguson's grieving mother. Juanita Young's drug-dealing son as far as he was concerned was the scum of Soundview. "Giuliani all, but concluded that he had it coming." With the support of her community, Ms. Young stayed strong and determined to see justice for her son. Ironically, Giuliani was diagnosed with prostate cancer while in office a few months later. Even after recovery, he continued to act like a gang leader and a bully. Karma is also a part of life and we'll surely await that wrath when it comes, too.

Giuliani is no leader. A liar and cheater who cheated on his wife for many years with his mistress, he does not possess the quality and honesty to be the leader of the greatest nation in the world. If Giuliani ever becomes the president of these United States, it will be the second coming of Hitler for black people. However, that shouldn't be the only reason why Giuliani shouldn't get elected. If you ask me, his political resume seems to be a one-liner, mayor of New York City. I still don't understand how a leader is being made out of Giuliani because of 9/11. It wasn't Giuliani, but an emergency plan that was devised after the bombing of The World Trade Center to deal with the city's emergencies. All that needed to be done during 9/11 was follow the plan. It's been alleged that Giuliani himself had no idea what the plan was initially. I would love to know exactly what qualifications that Giuliani possesses to run the nation other than being the mayor who ran a corrupted New York City.

Published articles reported appalling expression of the effective denial of basic democratic rights to working class and poor people, especially, but not only, the Black, Latino and immigrant populations, have divided New York City into two groups, the Haves and the Have-nots. Under the "stop and frisk" policies implemented by the Street Crime Unit years ago, tens of thousands have been thrown up against the wall and searched, based on suspicions every bit as flimsy as the one that led to the West African immigrant's death. Over seventy five percent of the victims of this policy have been Black and Latino. This policy was just another way for the NYPD to continue their operation as a gang to overtly abuse people while claiming that they're maintaining order.

To be fair to New York City, I must point out that the problem of police brutality across the USA is widespread and persistent, according to published reports. Thousands of documented individual complaints about police abuse are filed and reported each year and local authorities have to pay out millions of dollars to victims in damages after lawsuits are filed, which taxpayers always end up footing the bill. Records have shown that police officers have beaten and shot unresisting suspects; they have misused batons, chemical sprays and electro-shock weapons; they have injured or killed people by placing them in dangerous restraint holds. These officers are worse than the criminals on the streets that they're supposed to be protecting us from. Some of us are just lucky enough to be spared the wrath of these gang member officers around the country.

The overwhelming majority of victims in many areas are Black or Latino, while most police departments remain predominantly white. Police don't make a deserving effort to reach out to minority communities because they are looked at as villains by most officers. Thus relationship between the police and members of minority communities – especially young black and Latino males in inner city areas – are often strained, and racial bias is often reported or indicated as a factor in many instances of police brutality. Racial bias is evident in almost everything that has to do with the police departments around the country regarding abuse in minority communities in the urban areas in general.

Police officers are responsible for upholding the law and protecting the rights of all members of society. Their job is often difficult and sometimes dangerous, but most of them choose this profession at their own will. The danger affiliated with the job shouldn't justify the abuse that minorities are suffering at the hands of police. Experience from around the world shows that constant vigilance is required to ensure the highest standards of conduct-standards necessary to maintain public confidence and to meet national requirements.

This well-known published article acknowledged that in the USA, despite reform programs in several major police departments across the country, the authorities still failed to deal with police officers who have committed abuses in an effective manner. Police officers usually go unpunished for abusing citizens' rights even with evidence. The disciplinary sanctions imposed on officers found guilty of brutality are frequently unfair and inadequate, and officers are rarely prosecuted for excessive force against victims. The "blue code of silence" – in which officers diligently fail to report brutality or cover up abuses-commands widespread loyalty amongst officers, contributing to a dangerous climate of impunity. Although there has been some pressure placed on police departments to become more publicly accountable for misconduct in recent years through independent oversight mechanisms, these remain inadequate or completely absent in many areas, and continue to be despite the many incidences that have taken place with police. Only the federal government can attempt to derail this behavior through endless hours of investigation with un-cooperating police witnesses.

It seems more deliberate, but unfortunately there has not been any reliable national data on the excessive use of force by police, and most local reporting systems are spotty and often unreliable. Such data is essential to enable the authorities to take effective action. Since 1994, the federal government has been legally required to collect national data on police use of excessive force, but Congress has failed to provide the funding necessary for it to do so. The abuse of innocent minority victims is just not a priority at this time. Congress has more important issues to deal with like saving the whales and giving the president the green light to go to war under false pretenses. We have to pressure our elected congressman to approve funds for issues that affect our livelihood. These Congressmen need to be reminded about who put them in office to begin with, it's always the people and they need to be reminded.

Amnesty International believes that police forces throughout the USA must be made more accountable for their actions by the establishment of effective monitoring mechanisms. National, state and local police authorities should ensure that police brutality and excessive force are not tolerated: all allegations of police abuse should be promptly, fairly and independently investigated and those responsible brought to justice. Instead of simply paying compensation to victims, emphasis should be placed on stopping and preventing the abuses.

22

Another City Worst than New York

As bad as it may seem in New York City, we have another city that is worst when it comes to police shootings, and that city is none other than Detroit. According to published reports, police officers in Detroit, Michigan killed citizens at a much higher rate than police in any other big major US city. These FBI statistic findings were made public by the *Detroit Free Press*. The deadly shooting rate by police in Detroit was higher than New York City and Los Angles, the other two cities with a history of widespread police killings and brutality. Detroit had a murder rate of 0.92 fatal shootings per 100,000 citizens. The per capita murder rate in Detroit, however, is not greater than the number of people killed by NYPD Officers.

Detroit averaged close to ten fatal police shootings annually between 1990 and 1998, in a city where nearly one million people resided. Compared to New York with 7.3 million residents where the averaged number of fatal shootings per year was 28 during the same period—a rate of 0.39. The New York Police Department is still widely known as one of the most corrupted in the nation. The number of victims killed by the NYPD is over twice the amount killed in Detroit. Average in comparison with demographic measure can be deceptive.

The shootings in Detroit kept journalists at the *Detroit Free Press* and the *Detroit News* occupied for many years. Many exposés about the police shootings and subsequent cover-ups by internal police investigators have been published, as well as corruption by the Wayne County Prosecutor's Office and the Michigan State Police. There were detailed articles that exposed several cases of brutality and murder in which police officers killed or severely wounded senior citizens, teenagers and even the mentally ill. Most of these officers were exonerated after claiming they had fired in "self-defense." Self defense is always the excuse that police officers can claim after a shooting, even when there's no evidence that they were ever in any danger.

Thirty five officers in Detroit were cleared of wrongdoing in a city plagued by forty shootings over the course of five years. However, a minute number of four were charged with misdemeanors, and of the four, only one police officer was convicted and sentenced to jail. It didn't stop the city from settling a total number of six lawsuits filed by victims' families for a total sum of $8.6 million since 1995 even though police departments cleared their officers who shot those victims.

It has been acknowledged by former police executives and attorneys that officers feel they can definitely murder and terrorize city residents with impunity because they're seldom held accountable for their actions. The blame is mostly reverted on the dying victim while police try everything in their power to justify the shootings, instead of concluding the cause. The concoction of stories by police officers in Detroit is no different than those cops in New York City and the Los Angeles Police Department. They are usually assisted by investigators who try everything in their power to protect them. Eyewitnesses are usually avoided by these investigators and evidence overlooked, according to attorneys and former police executives.

"The failure of the Detroit Police Department to discipline its officers is intentional and deliberately indifferent to the rights of the citizens," retired Police Commander Clinton Donaldson, who ran the internal controls division from 1986 to 1994, stated in a documented lawsuit brought by an unarmed man who was shot by police.

On eight separate occasions and in eight different cases, officers claimed they fired because they felt their life was threatened when people approached them with guns, but autopsies in those cases found the victims were shot in the back. Still, no red flags were raised. Why? A simple answer can confirm that, the victims were black or a minority of some kind. One example of this was the case of Hong Leong in November 1997, a 40-year-old factory worker with a history of mental illness. Police officers John Borgens and James Pratt chased Leong's car into a dead-end street after he screeched his tires while rounding a corner. The police said Leong, apparently drunk, climbed out his car with a 12-gauge shotgun, fired into the air and yelled, "Go ahead and shoot me!" It was another made up lie because they knew they could get away with murdering a man who was a minority without any recourse.

Police claimed they shot Leong when he turned on them with the gun and aimed at them. He died of 12 to 16 shots to the back and the palm of one hand. He must've been running and shooting like a phantom cowboy from the Wild Wild West because ballistic tests revealed that his gun had never been fired. Even with this evidence, both homicide detectives and the Wayne County Prosecutor's office said the officers shot in self-defense. They must've been defending their right to go hunting for an Asian man in the middle of the night.

"I think they executed him and the department covered it up," said David A. Robinson, an attorney representing police victims, who worked thirteen years as a Detroit police officer. "An officer can literally get away with murder so long as he recites the magical incantation of "fearing for my life," or hides behind the magical talisman of the "dark, shiny object," Robinson said. Only a former police officer would know the magical words that cops are able to use to get away with murder. Mr. Robinson must've been fed up with his job and decided to fight the injustice he witnessed for thirteen years.

There have been cases where individual police officers have more than one fatal shooting to their "credit." Officer Eugene Brown, of the Detroit Police Department's Tactical Services Section, had killed three people and wounded six others during the first six years he worked for the police department. This behavior pattern never once warranted a termination because all his victims were minorities. He was given the green light to continue with his shooting rampage because the police department and prosecutors ruled Brown acted appropriately in every case.

Brown's blemished record prevented him from obtaining law enforcement jobs from other places, including the Los Angeles Sheriff Department, but the Detroit Police Department welcomed him with open arms and even allowed him to serve as a security guard for Mayor Dennis Archer and City Council members for several months.

On February 8, 1995, Brown killed 30-year-old Roderick Carrington with three gunshots fired within 15 seconds while his partner stood aside and watched the whole event without firing a single shot. Brown claimed that Carrington was charging at him with a knife. However, it wouldn't the last time that Brown would fatally shoot someone.

On September 21, 1996 Brown fatally shot twenty-year-old LaMar Grable close range with three shots to the chest and two bullets in the back. An obvious coward who hides behind his gun and badge, Brown lied about the incident and explained it away by saying that Grable was carrying a gun when he spotted him walking in the rain in the middle of the night. His vision was accurate enough to spot a gun, but no fire was ever returned. Grable simply ran away when he was challenged by Officer Brown and Brown got pissed and opened fire on him. Grable had no criminal record. The only fingerprints on the gun police said Grable was carrying belonged to Yost, Brown's partner. “The police claimed our client had a gun, but never did check into the serial numbers of the gun to see where it came from,” attorney Sheldon Miller said. Yost failed to show up for three scheduled depositions in the case and then refused to testify, pleading her Fifth Amendment right against self-incrimination. How Brown was able to continue to work as a cop is beyond me. Only corrupted police departments like Detroit, the NYPD and LAPD would allow this behavior to continue.

Brown was somehow cleared of any wrongdoing in court, but a court-appointed mediation panel recommended the city pay $750,000 to the family of LaMar Grable. However, the young man's family rejected the offer, and a lawsuit was filed.

City officials have repeatedly defended the actions of the police around the country. Detroit is only an example and a small percentage of a bigger problem, a problem that is too relevant in the black community. Detroit Police Chief Benny Napoleon and Wayne County Prosecutor John O'Hair said the figures comparing Detroit police shootings to other cities did not take into account how violent the city's criminals were. “There is a very violent element in our city,” O'Hair said in an interview with the *Free Press* after one of the shootings. “It is high-risk, and this is the element the police deal with.” He should’ve known that there was very violent element in his city because most of the violent offenders worked for the police department.

Detroit Mayor Dennis Archer defended police officers claiming they were not trigger-happy, and saying, “I have never met a police officer who fired a weapon who has felt good about it." He also defended the internal police investigators and Prosecutor O'Hair, saying, "the manner in which the cases have been handled thus far are consistent with good police practices." Then in an expression of conflict and impropriety avoidance, the mayor announced that his police department's Internal Control Bureau would conduct future investigations instead of Homicide detectives, claiming that there was no need to reopen old cases.

The Detroit news media has always been cognizant of the improper goings-on of the Detroit Police Department regarding brutality and official cover ups, but has generally written very little about it. The insurmountable number of innocent victims killed by police has forced their hands. Legitimate concerns are being raised about the police and prosecutor's office, and they are being discredited and the killings are undercutting the 25-year effort by city authorities to renovate the image of the police department. In the 1960s and 1970s the Detroit Police Department was one of the most notoriously violent police force in the country, particularly against minority youth. One police unit dubbed STRESS—Stop the Robberies, Enjoy Safe Streets—carried out the execution-style killings of more than a dozen black men in the span of a few years, according to published reports.

Coleman Young, who was elected the city's first black mayor in 1973 because of his pledge to disband the STRESS unit and to integrate the police force, soon found himself in accord with the police department after weaseling his way into winning an election by deception. However, Young and other Democratic officials ensured the appointment of black police chiefs and the recruitment of thousands of minority officers. The tunred of events started when social inequality was forced upon the residents of Detroit in the 1970s and 1980s—due in part to the mass layoffs and plant shutdowns in the auto industry. Detroit became one of the poorest big cities in America—Young reneged on his pledge to take away police power and started to once again strengthen the powers of the police and embraced the politics of law and order. His successor Dennis Archer has continued the same course after his election to office. As the *Free Press* acknowledged, "Race was a crucial factor in police shootings in the 1960s and 70s, with black residents being shot by white officers. But blue is the color that matters. Fatal shootings these days do not fall in apparent racial patterns. The officers are black and white, and the civilians are white, black and Asian alike."

Archer, a close political ally of the Clinton administration, led a city that was even more socially corrupt than Coleman Young left it. As the Detroit-area auto companies reaped tens of billions of dollars in profits, many of the city's working class areas were virtually uninhabitable due to years of chronic poverty, unemployment and budget cutting. Gambling became the new industry that helped impoverished the poor to levels unrecoverable. The blighted neighborhoods continued on a downward spiral as residents saw their paychecks disappear to support their new gambling habit. Those conditions did nothing but add to the encouragement of brute force on the part of the police as the crime rate rose in Detroit.

23

Racial Profiling

It's hard for some white people to even grasp the concept of racial profiling because they're not profiled on a daily basis because of their skin color. Not to say that all cops do this, but I know too many of them do it and get away with it. While mayor of New York City, Giuliani, enacted the "stop and frisk" law, which he knew damn well knew was going to affect only the minority groups, cops were given the liberty to stop and frisk anyone on the street as long as they felt there was some type of suspicion on their part or as they legally referred to it, probable cause. Probable cause to a lot of cops is "let's go out and frisk a bunch of niggers today, and we bound to get a few arrests." White people never stand to fight these laws because they understand fair and well that these laws don't affect them. Maybe some drunk, homeless white guy might get frisked after someone points a finger at him for a crime and even then, it's still less likely to happen.

The streets of Brooklyn, the Jamaica section of Queens, Washington Heights and many other parts of the Bronx is like a breeding haven for crooked cops. Hustlers rely heavily on these crooked cops for their daily hustle. It's not unusual for a cop to look the other way for a percentage of the hustlers' money. These cops are often not reported by these hustlers because of the deadly consequences that they might face. It's not right to deal drugs or commit other petty crimes on the streets, but it's even worse when cops are extorting people for the benefit of their own pockets at tax payers' expense.

Racial profiling has made it easy for these cops to go to court and get convictions. They're profiling us, but no one is profiling them. Internal Affairs only investigate cops with too many blemishes on their record. It usually takes years before anything draws a red flag and by then too many people have suffered or a simple resignation from the force allows a cop to get off Scott free from being prosecuted. Many of the cops in New York City are especially jealous of the rappers and other black entertainers in New York City. The young rappers are bold, brash and they wear their money on their sleeves and these "thirty thousand dollars a year" overzealous cops ain't having it. Why should they be busting their ass everyday and earning so little money? Well, they have no rapping talent for one and it's not like the NYPD salary is hidden from them before joining the force. These cops are modern day haters who look for any reason to embarrass a man in a better financial situation than they are.

Racial profiling has caused some disturbances in my own personal life as well. I was once pulled over on my way to work for no reason. When the police officer asked to search my BMW and I told him "no," he became angry and authoritative. Who the hell was I to say no to a cop? I knew my rights and I wasn't going to let him walk all over me. "If I search the car and find nothing, I'll let you go," he said. I anxiously wanted to get to work because I was a school teacher and I couldn't be late because I expected my students to be on time. I compromised my own civil rights for my students because this cop wanted to act like an ass. As he searched the car, I thought about the injustice that a simple badge allowed a man to bestow upon another man. Honestly, if I were a criminal, I probably would have harmed that cop for his actions because there was no reason for his search. After searching my car and found nothing, he simply laughed and told me to be on my way. I never went back to file a report on him because it would've taken too much work at the time. Unfortunately, my cell phone didn't have a camera then.

Situations like these make racial profiling unjust and unfair. If every black man who drives a nice car is suspected f being a drug dealer, then that means that every time a police officer approaches a black man in a nice car, he uses prejudice and the possibility of a serious deadly confrontation is possible and relevant. Reaching for a cell phone may warrant a bullet from him. I knew when the cop pulled me over that morning on my way to work, he wanted to find something and keeping his hand intimidatingly on his gun was a way to tell me if I didn't do what he wanted, he had the right to shoot me. I won't even go into the fact that he started questioning me about how I could afford my car like it was his fucking business.

Unfortunately, racial profiling is not only committed by white cops. Black police officers do it as well, but the approach is usually different. A black cop is more likely to differentiate between the types of black people they pull over. A street hustler is always in hustling mode as I was told by one cop. They'll try to hustle their way out of anything while the working man, usually gets pissed for being inconvenienced. Most white cops consider us all hustlers and they can't tell the difference as long as the common denominator is black or brown skin.

Racial profiling has hurt many people and taken many lives as well. The same prejudice that is used when a cop pulls a person of color over is the same prejudice feelings have these cops feeling threatened and unsafe in our presence. The likelihood of us carrying a gun is very high to them and for that reason they get trigger happy with total disrespect for black life. The case on the New Jersey turnpike involving state troopers is the best example of a cop using racial profiling to shoot at a group of young men for no reason other their skin. It's now illegal to do, according to the law, but we all know they have never stopped. Black people continue to be victims of racial profiling on the New Jersey turnpike everyday, and tickets are being handed out even when they're not warranted in order for the cops to cover their asses.

Cases like mine also take place all over New York City and other major cities. I've been pulled over hundreds of times illegally, but I've had to conform to a system that has taken away my rights completely because of my skin color. The situations, in most cases, have to be grave for the injustices to come light. Someone has to be shot in order for these cops to be investigated. In

New York City, civilians are usually given the run around when they try to file a report against cops. Police officers at the precinct in Jamaica New York are notoriously known for not turning in reports filed against their fellow officers for illegal behaviors.

Police officers across the country have made it a habit to rely solely on race to determine if a person is a criminal. Race has been used as the primary indicator for suspicious conduct and dangerous behaviors. The case of a 16-year-old black teenager shot by police in Indianapolis, Indiana while pedaling his bicycle in March 1993 is a great example of this. While most white teenagers enjoy the adolescent freedom of their youth while riding a bike in their neighborhood, young black men are considered fleeing felons by police officers. Not to say that some black teenagers don't use their bike as mean of transportation while conducting illegal activities, but now they're all suspects of illegal activities while riding their bikes because of a minority few

Members of minority groups are most likely to become victims of police brutality across the nation. The substantial amount of complaints filed every year by people of the minority community is a key factor that proves that social and economic inequalities that these people are subjected to maltreatment because of their social status. **Police activities often take place in low income neighborhoods and the disproportionate number of people associated to crimes due to survival will continue to affect the treatment of these folks by police.** There's no absolute certain data on the unfair treatment of people in the hood, but evidence of police bias and discriminatory treatment of minorities by police has been documented by citizen complaints, in court and other commissions of inquiry. It's no surprise that African-Americans and other minority groups have no confidence in the police departments around the country. Reported abuses often involved racist language during an arrest, unjustified shootings such as the ones cited in this book, false arrests, and total maltreatment of people at the hands of police. What gives for a people without a voice?

The problem used to be confined to the inner cities, but not anymore. A case of a plainclothes Boston police officer driving through a suburban town known as Randolph in Massachusetts depicts the fact that police officers in suburbia are using racial profile as well. While driving his Cadillac, Escalades, the police officer was pulled over and before he was given the chance to identify himself as a police officer, he was beaten and taken to jail without committing as much as an offense by Randolph police officers. Randolph, a city widely known for its racist and corrupt officers only offered an apology to the officer wrongly arrested.

There have also been long standing brutality by law enforcement officers towards people of Latin American origin near the US-Mexican border and in other states with large immigrant populations such as New York, California, Texas and Florida. Even Native Americans have suffered the brunt of police brutality on their reservations.

Black women in suburban, Chicago who lived in a town know as Riverdale where the proportion of Black has been rising as of lately, have reported assault by white police officers in the mid- 1990's. The documented case of Linda Billups was widely published when she was stopped by police while driving home from church with her four young children back in September of 1993. She was allegedly roughly handled by police officers, arrested and charged with several trumped up offenses, including assaulting an officer, a common charge by officers to justify their illegal actions. All charges were later dropped, but the woman faced humiliation in front of her children, something that's forever irreparable. At least eight other black women were assaulted in separate incidents in two years, including Diane Overstreet who was kicked, thrown to the ground and subjected to racial slurs for allegedly running through a red light. The thirty full-time officers in that own at the time were all white male, according to published reports.

24

The Imbalance of Race in the NYPD

In recent years, many police departments around the country have put more effort in recruiting minority police officers, but there is still a great disparity in the numbers. Cultural diversity has been introduced and racial sensitivity training programs are made available to the officers now. It is alleged that these training are thrown out the window the minute these officers leave the training centers. White police officers often complain about attending these trainings because the prejudice and racism is a part of them and nothing can change that. The racist officers are not rooted out because the system is not fool proof and people live everyday to get what they want, even if it's a job that they don't like.

To add insult to injury, often times the recruited minority officers don't even have the opportunity for advancement within the police departments because of their racist subordinates. The departments are primarily made of the "good ole boys" and breaking that wall is often a task in itself. There has been troubling evidence of discrimination against minority officers in almost every police department around the country. There have been numerous lawsuits filed on behalf of minority officers seeking promotions alleging racial discrimination. Minority officers are even sometimes subjected to racial slurs while on duty or completely overlooked for well deserved promotions because of their race. A recent case of this discrimination was when a jury awarded four million dollars in May of 1998 to a former deputy marshal who had been passed over for a promotion because he was black.

Another problem that befalls many of our police departments is the wide gap between the composition of inner city communities and the police force. It's no hidden secrets that the majority of police officers in most major cities are white. However, the people who are often arrested and subjected to daily harassment are often black. Just because someone is forced to attend sensitivity or racial diversity training, it doesn't mean that their racial attitude or prejudice is taken away. Racism is deeply rooted and some people keep it at the forefront in their daily lives when dealing with people of another race that they don't like. Some might even see their badge and gun as repatriation for being forced to work and live with that hated group. Psychologically speaking, we are fooled everyday by liars and cheaters and some people are very professional and great at what they do. Wallstreet offers the best of them and the NYPD is in second place fighting for the top spot.

A lot of police officers often have to be great liars in court in order to convince the prosecutor, judge or jury that they're right in their actions. The lying usually starts at the academy and escalates to levels beyond control when a corrupted police officer has been able to fall through the cracks. There's no psychological assessment that can root out racism and prejudice completely. Everyone, most of the time, acts under false pretense to obtain something that is controlled by somebody else and police officers are no different.

The reason why the detrimental behavior is pervasive is because the "blue code of silence" adheres to it and there's nothing that can be done to combat it. Minority police officers are often threatened when they take a stance against the brutality that they witness within the police departments and sometimes it is so polarized that some of them choose to leave law enforcement all together. The majority of police officers around the country are white, which places the minority officers at their mercy. A black officer most of the time, have to tolerate the destructive behavior of his fellow white officer because he can face death at any given moment and he has to rely on that maniacal officer for backup in a deadly situation.

I've talked to many black officers who have expressed their disdain for the way some of their white counterparts have acted towards black people in the hood. However, the fear of being blackballed keeps them from reporting the ill-acting officers. It's not by chance that Hollywood depicts these racists officers for what they are in films that portray racist behaviors that we sometime feel are beyond comprehension. Some of these officers do exist and Mark Furman of the Los Angeles Police Department was one of those officers. The N word was a daily part of his vocabulary and we can only imagine how much pain he has inflicted on innocent Black victims while he was a police officer, yet there were no repercussions for his inappropriate actions. Instead, he's rewarded with book deals and speaking engagements that propelled him to the daily list of millionaires in America. That ultimately sent the message that it's okay to be racist while on the force as long as one is not overt with it. The perpetrators are usually painted as liars in court, so it's easy for these cops to exhibit these behaviors on a daily basis.

The NYPD's positions of power all belong to white officers. Of the 699 officers at captain or above, hired by the NYPD, only 19 of them are black. That is just about a little over two percent, which is alarming considering that twenty five percent of New York City is made up of Black people. Only 5.7 percent of the sergeants in the NYPD are Black. Out of the 59 officers in the aviation unit, only one is Black. While the NYPD advertises opportunities for its officers to potential recruits, it is clear-cut that those opportunities are limited to mostly White officers. White men from the suburb dominate the academy each class at the NYPD because there's no residency requirement. These suburbanites are more likely to be involved in shootings because the stigma of fear attached to the city is never absent from their mind.

Mayor Giuliani's own police chief claimed that Giuliani did not back several initiatives to accelerate the integration of the police force in New York City when he became mayor. Fewer Black officers were hired during Giuliani's tenure as mayor and very little effort was spent in promoting minority officers. Giuliani's record also reflects a regression in minority promotion. The Bloomberg administration has not fared any better.

I know this may sound redundant because you have heard it throughout this book, but racism with the NYPD does not take place only against civilians. The NYPD continues to be run by the "good ole boy" network and the Black officers feel the brunt of their racist practices everyday. The personnel record of the NYPD reflects the illegal practice of promotion based on race, nepotism, but not experience. Black officers with seniority are often overlooked for promotions.

According to their own personnel statistics, every special department of the NYPD has lagged behind in promoting minority officers. The Emergency Service Unit comprised of 500 officers has only 37 Black officers; The Mounted Unit has 3 Black officers out of 120 plus officers; Major Case Detective Squad has 3 Black officers out of more than 43; The Harbor Unit only has 2 Black officers out of more than 150 officers; The Street Crime Unit shows the strongest number of Black officers of 46 out of more than 290 officers. Blacks are underrepresented in every aspect of the NYPD. The NYPD is only interested in foot soldiers when they recruit from the Black community. Their campaign about advancement within the NYPD is very deceptive to the young Black men and women who sign up for a career.

Black officers are discouraged at every turn. Civil Service Exams are used to keep Black officers from being promoted. Even those Black officers who score higher than their fellow White officers on these exams are overlooked for promotions. Officer David Leader, the only Black pilot who works for the NYPD had to file a discrimination complaint against them because he had been denied training because of his race. So many Black officers are frustrated with the NYPD promotion system that they are willing to turn in their badge and walk away from the job altogether. The NYPD creates a discouraging environment for Black officers. Even a former White chief called the unequal access to prominence within the NYPD for Blacks “a quiet shame." Too many Black officers have been sold on false promises while at the police academy, according to a couple of officers. "What they tell us at the academy as far as equal opportunity is completely different than what actually happens once a person becomes a police officer," said one officer who's been with the department for over twenty years.

Despite the fact that so many of the elite units of the NYPD serve major minority communities, they are consisted of entirely White men. The NYPD was on notice for creating segregated elite units for so many years. The "spoil system" also keeps Blacks from earning promotion and perks from the NYPD. The lack of Black officers in top positions makes it difficult for Black officers to have access to the spoil system. Nepotism is rampant in the NYPD and only those with family members at the top have access to cushioned positions. Although I'm not a cop, it's quite frustrating to write about this because it also exists in every Civil Service job in New York City. This way of conducting business has a trickle down affect throughout the city and Black people are mostly the victims. This racist practice can be a whole book on its own.

Even today, the NYPD still lacks in the department's effort to hire minority officers. Other problems stem from the fact that the NYPD is overtly racist towards its Black officers, and also has a system in place that disproportionately limits the advancement of Black officers. There appears to be existing barriers at every turn for Black police officers at the NYPD, and thus will continue to create an imbalance of power, race and fairness. Less than ten percent of New York Police Department officers are Black.

25

Gay Men and Lesbians

Though I'm not an expert of gay and lesbian issues, I feel it is only fair to point out the harassment that the Gay and Lesbian community has also suffered at the hands of police. The gay and lesbian community has suffered greatly in many areas. Often times, police are non-responsive to their complaints of homophobic attack crime against that community because of rampant prejudice attitude. In some instances members of the community are met with physical and verbal abuse by police because of their chosen lifestyle. Homophobia has long been a problem with police departments throughout the United States, and police agencies claim that they have tried to undertake the problem in police ranks and training. As reported by the National Coalition of Anti-Violence Programs (NCAVP), there has been a great disturbing increase in reported incidents of homophobic violence by law enforcement officers since 1997.

It's one thing to be gay, but to be black and gay is double jeopardy, not in the legal sense. Responsive officers don't react positively to homosexuality when they're called to a scene. The first threat usually noted by them is the presence of a black person. Those people right away are subjected to the cruel treatment or racism existed in these police officers' minds, but when it's found out that they are gay, the maltreatment is usually twice as unbearable. While some police departments have tried to improve their relations with the Gay and Lesbian community by recruiting more gay and lesbian police officers, those officers are reported to have endured cruel, malicious, and hateful attitudes from their fellow officers.

In New York City, improvements to victim responses could only be reported due in part to the efforts of the Gay and Lesbian Anti-Violence Project accompanying victims to report crimes at the police stations as reported by them. They have to play the role of watchdogs to safeguard members of their community. The AVP also regularly take part in police training and gay and lesbian sensitivity programs to ensure that they are being dealt with in a fair manner. Their participation did not guarantee absolute fair treatment, because the problem is still ongoing. The Christopher Commission in 1991 in Los Angeles reported widespread discrimination within the Los Angeles Police Department toward gay and lesbian officers. After a lawsuit brought on by a gay former LAPD officer in 1993, the LAPD in their effort to save face, started recruiting officers from the Gay and Lesbian community and adopted other measures to combat discrimination. Those measures aren't foolproof because the LAPD have a poor record of citizen abuse at the hands of police. The LAPD continues to response poorly to victims reporting homophobic hate crimes, according to the Gay and Lesbian Anti-Violence Project. The response to crime against African-Americans is even worst.

The police have long played the role of antagonist against many discriminated groups. According to reports, there are some areas of selective enforcement of laws to target the gay and black community. For example, civil rights advocates in May 1998 reported that LAPD officers were selectively enforcing laws to harass gay men and women, and that included the entrapment of gay men into committing illegal sexual acts in public. Also, complaints were filed in 1997 in Maryland, according to published reports, that police in Maryland were inciting gay men to breach the state's discriminatory anti-sodomy law, which prohibits homosexuals from having oral sex and other unnatural practices in private. However, the same law didn't pertain to heterosexuals. Heterosexuals could sodomize each other as much as they want without recourse. One can't help but wonder how such laws would be enforced in the privacy of one's home?

26

Probability of Arrest

Of course, the probability of arrests for black men is much higher because they're harassed three times as much as any other groups. As I mentioned earlier, New York City enacted a law where the cops can at anytime demand to "stop and frisk" people based suspicions. This is an open door policy for harassment and abuse of the badge. Rights are being violated on a daily basis and the victims have no choice because a charge of disorderly conduct is enough for a person to end up in the back of a police cruiser for more harassment to come at the station. Most people just allow the cops to humiliate them to save themselves even more headache.

The chances for arrest does not increase just in New York City alone, it is across the country. My own personal experience was nightmarish. While driving my BMW again from New York to Boston, I was pulled over for DWB (Driving While Black) in Rhode Island by a state trooper. I was confident he pulled me over because of the color of my skin because there were three other cars in front of me and two behind me and we were all doing the speed limit. When the cop pulled out from his hiding place from the overpass under a bridge, he went directly after me cutting off the two drivers behind me. After checking my license and registration to make sure the car was properly registered and that I was the owner, he still wasn't satisfied. "Why was I pulled over?" I ask. No reason was given. "Do you mind if I search your car?" He answered my question with a question of his own. It was a response I grew accustomed to from them. I've never been afraid of a badge or gun, "what for?" I asked. "Because I want to," he answered while trying to shield his badge from view. "I guess you must want me to wait here while you get a search warrant," I said back to him.

It was a test of will between two people and the cop knew that he had no right to search my car. Soon after, another trooper pulled up behind him and the odds were no longer in my favor. The first cop who looked as soft as cotton suddenly developed this base in his voice when his back-up arrived. I was still undeterred from my position because it was daylight and if they were going to do something, they would've had to do it in front of other passersby. I tried to dial my friend's number on my cell phone so that I could have audio proof of any attack they were planning against me. After sitting around for about a half hour, one of the cops came up to me and said "look, you let us search your car and if we don't find anything, you can be on your way." I became even angrier and I knew out of uniform and without the badge neither cop stood a chance against me. I could tell that these guys were the laughingstock of their high school class. Suddenly, they're able to use authority because the police department afforded them that right. Against my principle, and the fact that I had nothing to hide, I allowed the two cowards to go through my car because I really needed to get to my destination. I drove home angry the whole way. When I tried to file a complaint against those cops, I was given the run around.

That day the probability of arrest for me was very high because those cops had really pushed my buttons and I came close to giving them a piece of my mind, which would have given them reason to charge me with, again, "disorderly conduct." Another similar situation happened in New York City with a crooked cop named John Hofman from the precinct in Jamaica, New York. It is common practice for cops and ticket agents who work for the City of New York to write bogus parking tickets to meet their quota. Investigative News reporters have uncovered and exposed many of these people. John Hofman was writing me parking tickets even when my car was not present. The only way I found out about the tickets was when they arrived in the mail at my house. When I went to court to fight those tickets, the judge told me it was my word against an officer's word. I was told that I needed solid proof to have the tickets dismissed. Even with an airline ticket proving that I was nowhere near New York City, still, the magistrate told me that I could've left my car with someone. I wanted set up a camera to videotape this cop to catch him in action, but it was time consuming. When I tried to go a different route to file a complaint against the officer, nobody at the precinct would give me the telephone number for Internal Affairs. It was no coincidence that I was getting those tickets by the same cop. I once confronted him about a bogus ticket he was writing for another car, and I became a target for him ever since. These are the types of cops who work for the NYPD. I still carry the proofs of his fictitious tickets with me. Those tickets cost me close to a thousand dollars.

You're probably wondering how that situation would've increased the probability of arrest for me, right? Just imagine that an officer was unjustly writing you $115.00 parking tickets for no reason, what would your reaction be if you saw that officer? These are some of the basic things that officers do because they know that they can get away with it. They abuse their authority and they cheat the regular citizens because they can, and nobody ever tries to put a stop to it. I'm sure I can come up with twenty more scenarios that are more extreme, but why should I have to go through that when an officer is supposed to be a trusted public servant? Some people just don't know what little it takes for a police officer to arrest a black man or any man for that matter.

I may not have been able to prove that he lied in court, but I can expose him for the liar he is in this book. The pen is mightier than the sword and I'm just glad I have the ability to use my pen to expose injustice. Hopefully, someone in Jamaica will read this book and will take notice of my situation and perhaps we might be able to prove that this officer has demonstrated this pattern of behavior against more than one victim. We have to be vigilant in our search for truth against these lying officers. They're going to spoil the whole bunch if we don't get rid of the few bad apples.

27

Technology and Police Watch

In order to help decrease police brutality, we have to collectively work as a group. Technology has made it easier for the government to keep tabs on all of us and for police departments to identify suspects and criminals from all walks of life. We, the civilians have to use the same technology to help protect our fellow citizens from rogue cops as well. It doesn't take much to capture abuse on camera. As I mentioned before, we all know even with the evidence of videotape footage of abuse that these cops walk away Scott free from being prosecuted, but we must keep at it.

Something as simple as a cell phone can bring about justice to a victim's family. Most of us have the technology of recording events such as police abuse at our disposal, but we get so caught up in shock and awe while watching the injustice take place that we forget about the technology that we carry on our waist or in our pockets or purses sometimes. We have to be diligent in the hood in order for us to maintain order and justice. I'm not advocating that we use our cell phones to follow the cops around to record their mishaps, but we must raise our awareness in the interest of our people in order to protect our well being. Your phone cameras don't have to be used for only unjust police beatings of victims, it can also be used to get rid of the bad elements in your community as well. While it may be harder to convince a jury to convict a cop after he just unloaded forty one shots into a victim, it's not that hard to convince that same jury to convict the drug pushers who are trying to derail your kids from a good education.

We can help the police while helping ourselves as well. One of the main reasons that these cops are able to justify their actions in court is because we do have some bad elements in our community, but why give them all the easy ammunition they need. Let's help them clean up our neighborhood in a dutiful way so that when they act inappropriately, we can say that we've been there behind you from the start and there is no reason for the excessive force or abuse when it's not necessary.

It's never right to say that all police officers are bad, but the amount of bad people becoming police officers seems to be increasing by the day. There are officers out there who figure that it's easier to be a criminal with a badge and a gun. And these are the officers that we need to keep off the streets just like the criminals we don't want on our streets and in our communities.

I would like to encourage people to get to know their cell phones and don't hesitate to pay the extra money to get a phone that comes with a video camera because that camera might even save you from doing time behind bars because of a crooked cops allegation against you. One thing that I always do now when I get pulled over by a cop for a traffic infraction or anything for that matter is that I turn on my video camera to record the events as they happen because sometimes you just never know. The camera on your cell phone can be a very important tool when used accordingly and we shouldn't allow the law to only work one way. We have to start looking after each other because Reverend Al can't look out for every single one of us. Let's make sure these cops do what is in their job descriptions and not what they feel they can get away with because they have a badge and a gun. They're sworn to uphold the law let's hold them up to it, and only the citizens can make sure that they're not breaking the law.

New York City is in great need of an empowered citizen review board that can make recommendations to the mayor for serious consideration to help monitor the corrupt officers in the department, and we can help them by providing the evidence needed for their recommendation. You don't have to be a black nationalist to do your duty as a citizen. The days of Eldridge Cleaver, Huey Newton and Stokely Carmicheal are long gone, but let's not allow them to be forgotten. These men cared about their communities and we need to continue their fight for justice and equality.

The police department in New York City is getting help from many different angles. Picture cameras are set up at various different traffic lights to help finance the City's police department. Tickets for red light violations bring in millions of dollars to the city because of these cameras. It's about time the citizens of New York and the rest of the country become just as vigilant in rooting out police brutality and abuse. Your cell phone camera is just as effective as those cameras that capture a violator running through a red light, use it. Let these cops know that they're being watched and don't allow them to intimidate you. Work collectively. They have no right to confiscate video footage from your private cell phone. Let the world see them in action. Send your footage to the media and let the judges and jury see the evidence needed to put some of these scumbags away. Scumbag is a common term often used by cops when referring to criminals, so it's only appropriate that I use the same term to refer to these criminal cops who are a disgrace to police departments everywhere. Your video footage can shield you from the witness stand. You can anonymously report misbehavior by simply emailing your footage to your local news station.

28

Hiding Behind "Procedure"

One of the most common excuses that officers use to defend their improper actions in any kind of altercations with the public that resulted in death or other types of abuse or brutality is that they were following procedure. Procedure is not really defined to the public, so most of us don't understand the meaning of that word. However, someone at the police academy must've taught them to say that they're following procedure. If procedure allows the police to take the life of innocent unarmed victims without justification, perhaps the public should be made aware of its definition. A lot of victims around the country have lost their lives because of procedure and procedure usually goes hand in hand with due process in court.

A family shouldn't have to wait until they go to a hearing, in most cases only if the cops are indicted, to hear what the procedure is that the cops are supposed to be following. Agonizing over a love one's death is one of the most painful things that people have to do and having to wait to hear a judge ask a police defendant to define the department's procedure in court just prolongs the grieving process for family members. We have to be weary of words like procedure being thrown around by crooked cops because they know it can be used as a defense. A uniform code of behavior should be made available to the public so that these officers are aware of the fact that the public knows what procedure should be followed in a particular situation.

Is it procedure to give police officers involved in a shooting days and sometimes weeks to concoct a story or a defense before investigating them? Alleged criminals caught committing crimes are usually questioned minutes and sometimes seconds after the crime has been committed before they even arrive at the police station. And sometimes they're questioned against their will without the presentation of an attorney or their Miranda rights read to them. Why do cops get a different treatment?

I would love to know the procedure that allowed cops to unload forty one bullets at Amadou Diallo while nineteen of them pierced holes throughout his body. There must be such a procedure because the cops who murdered him never lost their jobs and was acquitted of any wrongdoing in the case. Two of those officers are still working for the force and one of them is not satisfied that he got to keep his job after murdering a man in cold blood, but he's now fighting to get his service revolver back so he can return to the streets to kill more innocent victims.

I'm learning that procedure allows cops to kill innocent victims and they might lose the right to their service revolver, but there's always an administrative desk job waiting at the precinct for them while the victims' families grieve. Procedure is a more important word than we think.

They must've also been following procedure when they unloaded the fifty bullets that killed Sean Bell and damn near killed two of his friends. I don't know what procedure is anymore. Perhaps procedure is for police officers to concoct extra assailants when they have no defense in a situation in order to justify unloading and reloading a gun while there was never any imminent danger. I'm just trying my hardest to understand what the word procedure mean as it relates to police. Following procedure somehow seem to only affect people of color. Procedure can also be the right to harass black men who drive through predominantly white neighborhoods. I couldn't find an officer to explain the word procedure to me, so I'm just trying to attach a meaning to it based on their actions towards black and brown people.

I became a victim of procedure as I mentioned before when a white man decided that he could get away with murdering his wife in the Roxbury section of Boston and lie to police that he was mugged by black men. Oh procedure had me thrown up against the wall and searched for no reason at all because I was a suspect based on this white man's vague lying description of a black man who killed his pregnant wife. The Charles Stewart case has been silent in Boston for years now because Black people didn't commit the heinous crime. However, because of procedure black people were put through the ringer.

Basically, procedure means that the cops have the right to do whatever the hell they want to do and any white person can walk into any precinct and fabricate a story about black people and we'll be subjected to procedural searches and illegal behaviors by police. Not only that, if there's more than two black men in a group, police can also open fire at will because procedure will get them off in court. Procedure gives them the right to say that "they fear for their life."

I've warned people in the introduction of my book Neglected Souls, about carrying their cell phones on their waistband, but I feel the need to reiterate why they might just fall victim to a shooting and lose their life because procedure allows cops to shoot at black men carrying cell phones on their waist. Amadou Diallo had no idea which procedure he was to follow or the cops were following when they lit up his body with nineteen bullets. In a barrage of bullets, the man lost his life because procedure allowed the cops to consider his life less important because of the color of his skin. Sean Bell lost his life because procedure allows cops to surround black men driving at night with their guns drawn without properly identifying themselves as police officers. Procedure also takes away the rights of black people to decide whether or not they should try to escape danger when they're under fire. That's procedure alright.

29

Getting Sucked In By the Blue Entity

Just like anything else, the police department is an entity, an entity that is known and supported around the world. Only an entity can gain international respect by everybody around the world. Entities are easily recognized and most people are aware of the best entities created or built. Michael Jordan has become a conglomerate and an entity, but his power is only for marketing and gaining purposes. The police are known as an entity that is feared, respected and known for upholding the law that protects the people. However, that entity has its own rules and regulations that have to be followed by its members. And when those rules and regulations are not followed, as a stockholder, you may lose big. Let's be definitive here, we're all stockholders in the police department because they are compensated by public taxes.

Let's consider ourselves stockholders while the patrolmen, commissioner, and mayor are part of the board of directors. The board of directors makes the rules and since they know how to generate interest in their entity, they make sure that those rules are followed and regulated in every way. In America, it seems that one of the rules that was made up for this entity was that black life is worth less than white life and if a situation should arise, the stockholders are less likely to lose if a black life is taken. Under those rules and guidelines also falls practice. And the practice is that they always stick together as an entity no matter what.

I recently spoke to a couple of officers who left me astonished after revealing to me what goes on during a police investigation. It would be unfair to rat out these officers because that's one of the rules of the police department that you don't rat out fellow officers even if they're wrong. What shocked the hell out of me was, according to these officers, that if a police shooting takes place and there's more than one officer involved or at the scene, all the officers are expected to discharge their service revolver if one of them shoots for whatever reason. They're often scolded and told that they're not part of the team if they don't partake in the shooting. Their revolver is usually checked for ballistics and even if discharging their revolver was not warranted, they're expected to discharge because they have to work as a unit. "United we stand divided we fall" is the mantra by which they operate.

In essence, every new police officer who takes the oath to protect and serve falls under the guise of the blue entity because their life depend on it for survival on the job. Every new officer is sucked in right away because it is widely known that police officers stick together, and only in rare cases that a police officer might testify against his fellow officers. The blue entity has remained strong because of the unwritten rule of loyalty to the police department. Every new recruit understands that his or her life may depend on the allegiance of his fellow officer. Along with the oath to protect and serve the public, is also the oath to protect and serve their fellow officers at all costs. They have to protect each other in every situation and serve as alibis and witnesses to fabricate ways out of wrongdoings.

The impurity of the police forces around this country is almost scary considering that these people have enough fire power to hold a major city hostage. It's clearly understood why mayors usually rally behind their police departments. They understand clearly the amount of power these men have. The power of this entity is underestimated by most and it's managed to stay that way because scrutiny would force them to relinquish power. Police officers are often praised because of their bravery, but not every police officer is brave. Within the entity also stand a lot of cowards who hide behind the strength of the entity and their intention most of the time is nothing short of malice. It has to be considered malicious for a human being to shoot at another unarmed human being over thirty one times knowing that it only takes one shot to keep a charging suspect from inflicting any kind of pain or injury.

There's a huge difference between subduing and killing. Police officers are trained to shoot accurately, but most of the time they aim to kill when the victims are black or brown. The blue entity has made it okay to forgo the training when the encounter is with a person of color. I'd be hard pressed to find as many unarmed white victims shot more than twice by police officers during altercations. As a matter of fact, I searched all over for similar cases where white unarmed victim were shot multiple times without justification and I could only find a tiny fraction compared the amount of black victims, and most of the time the white victims were armed.

I don't want this to be one-sided and say that only white officers are killing black unarmed victims. The entity has created something that's becoming systemic, fear of black people. Black police officers are no longer able to relate to their fellow black men after graduating from the police academy. The "I'm one of them now" mentality gradually takes effect and suddenly they don't feel comfortable in their black surroundings anymore. It's fair to say that only a minority few feel like this and most of the time they end up finding themselves wrapped in shooting controversies such as the Sean Bell shooting.

Another thing that this entity has been able to create is the separated state of mind amongst black men. Haitian, Jamaican and other West Indian officers are made to feel that African-Americans are more dangerous than other Black people. However, the reality is that all Black people are subjected to the same maltreatment and injustice at the hands of officers. There's no indication that a Black person is of West Indian descent when he encounters a white officer or any police officer for that matter. The first thing that is relevant to them is the skin color. A great example of this was the shocking sodomy of Abner Louima who's Haitian, the killing of Amadou Diallo who was from West Africa and the murder of Sean Bell who was African-American. The common denominator in all three cases was their skin color, which was Black. Their heritage was irrelevant at the time of the abuse.

The entity has managed to create the best division of all amongst Black men. There are more prejudices amongst Black people than any other group. The colonization mindset has set us back as a total race and the entity capitalizes on it at every turn. We must not allow ourselves to be divided and conquered so easily.

The entity is not stupid, the entity also realized how powerful that African-Americans and Black people as a whole can be. The trendsetters of the world are found in the ghettos of America. Black people are emulated all over the world from their music to fashion and the entity understands that casting a dark cloud over Black people is the only way to keep them in check. I've even been sucked in by the entity because I should have never said "dark cloud." I'm conditioned to believe that everything dark is associated with evil, but most evil deeds seem to carry a light shadow most of the time. Iraq and many other areas of the world are great examples of this lurking evil.

30

Media Portrayals and Stereotypes of Black Folks

The portrayal of Black people has always been a problem with the American mainstream media. If it's propaganda to have the whole world believe that we're mostly criminal, then they're doing themselves a disservice as well. Despite the fact that so many stereotypes and stigmas are attached to Black people, many people of other ethnicities manage to love our culture and some even copy and live it. I'm not going to give credence to imbecility by talking about what it is that the media has done to create such a distorted image of us, but I will focus on is the fact that we are the most resilient group of people on this planet. I doubt if any other race could've gone through what we went through and still manage to be strong.

Despite all that we went through and the barriers created to keep us oppressed and desolate for so long, we have always found the strength to crack open a few doors. The wonderful thing about cracking these doors opened is that we usually master whatever it is that we were barred from to begin with. We can take education for example, most of our great grandparents were never given the chance to learn how to read because of the threat they posed intellectually to the rest of the country and the world, supposedly. Despite the hurdles, a few of the slaves managed to get together and started "each one teach one" and before we knew it the Historically Black Colleges and Universities were sprouting up all over the south, the most racist parts of the country. The colleges brought us the Tuskegee Airmen, Dr. Martin Luther King, Frederick Douglas, Booker T Washington, W.E.B. Du Bois and many more with capabilities to go on to attend Harvard University to earn post graduate degrees. We are definitely capable.

Black people have only been limited because those limits were imposed on them a long time ago. For some reason some of us never dismissed those limitations from our mind. Even though society would like us to believe that racism is nonexistent, we understand that now it takes a new shape and form. One of the most effective of them all is institutional racism. There's no sure way to fight it and it will continue to exist until the generation of the "good ole boys" are gone for good. It could be two or three generations from now because we all know that those sentiments are passed on. However, with new generations come a new way of thinking and one day we will get to the point where skin color will be the least of our concern. And when that day comes, America will finally be proud of all of its citizens.

The mere thought of denied access or the existence of a glass ceiling based on race, and not capability and ability, can cripple a child until he reaches manhood.

Children are very perceptive and they start to develop certain behavior patterns based on the way that they are treated or the image that is created for them. The media plays a crucial role in developing the sense of worth of every black child. The media has so far demonstrated their appreciation mostly for professional black athletes, entertainers and black art form that depicts poverty and the underbelly of being black. It wasn't until Senator Barack Obama hit the political scene that the white media has shown so much affection towards a black man. Sure he's not the first Ivy League educated brother to have accomplished so much, but they chose him only because it's about time for change. And thank God for his good looks and charisma. It's still a little premature to judge whether or not he will be destroyed by the same media who created this megastar out of him.

Those good ole boys will be weeded out to make way for the new independent thinkers, and only then will little Black boys feel worthy of becoming something other than the portrayals that they see on television, in the newspapers and magazines. I especially would like to thank Senator Obama for giving our youth a chance. Though many of us will still find reasons to disconnect ourselves to the charismatic senator, and the media plays a big part in that as well. His presence was long overdue. Obama is like the messiah that young black men have needed for a long time. I'm just glad and thankful that we now finally have someone to represent us who's not vilified for his color and his stance as a black man on political issues and other issues that affect people's lives in general. I can't say that Reverend Al and the good Reverend Jesse Jackson are not appreciated, but they don't have the charismatic affect that Obama has on the media, and their academic resumes don't reflect Harvard University and suma cum laude. As a black man, nothing less than Harvard will do in the media. The scrutiny that we undergo is twice as tough. The reverends, with their failed efforts, opened the door to make Obama feel that he at least stands a chance to compete for the presidential office. I'm sure if we took away Obama's complexion from the equation he would win the presidency by a landslide.

The media too, has played a role in separating black people. The grassroots effort of Senator Obama in the black community has not been expounded on enough to connect him to the community. People like Reverend Al Sharpton, though we appreciate his efforts, he always plays devil's advocate and want us to challenge the new black leaders on the issues. While it may be a good idea to make sure that that black candidates don't take our votes for granted, but Sharpton himself had no political credential when he decided to run for the presidency a few years ago. Just like Jesse Jackson, Reverend Al ran on hope and to help open doors for the future young black men who aspire to one day become president.

Unlike his predecessors, Barack Obama brings a sense of reality more than hope to his campaign and young black dreamers as a whole. He's a warrior for change and he doesn't make his color or people the main political platform for his campaign. Really, who would win the presidency doing that? Obama is not the only ray of light emerging on the political scene to inspire young black children, the governor of Massachusetts, Mr. Deval Patrick is also a very inspirational man to young black men, and he did not allow his race to create a barrier for him from the governorship. It's time for new leadership in the black community and America as a whole and some of us are just elated that little boys will have more than flamboyant characters to emulate. I'm also thankful that one day when I have a son, he will feel that there is no limit on what he can do with his life. My daughter has already made it clear to me.

Most Black people probably feel that they're very distant relatives of Obama because of his upbringing and family background. The media has managed to create separatist mindset amongst black people, those of the elite and those of the less fortunate. The two sides usually have a hard time getting along because most of the time, the urban dialect is the representation of the common bond and when a black person removes himself from it, they end up losing the true bond of brotherhood due to ignorance and media manipulation. We have to start recognizing that our common heritage doesn't necessarily equate to common intelligence, drive, determination, will, zeal and goal. We as black people, have to realize that America is a capitalist society and only as a competitor will we erase racism by demonstrating that we can compete on every level. And only then will the roots of racism start to erode and the new leaders will emerge and America will start to embrace all its citizens equally.

I find it weird that Black people connected to Bill Clinton because of the hardship he faced in his life and his apparent smooth connection to a saxophone. In reality, the Clinton administration did very little for Black people and Black countries around the world. "Clinton is the closest we'll ever have to a Black president," is one of the most common phrases heard around the hood. Nothing in Clinton's life signify his connection to black people other than his humble beginnings. Black people have a hard time accepting or connecting to other intelligent and educated Black folks because of our own lack of sense of worth. I hope Obama is the rebuilding process and I hope that Black people can embrace him for the true person that he is and for the uplift that he has given to the race as a whole, not just because of the media but also his true nature and intentions. Some of us, however, know better because we encounter many Barrack Obamas in the hood everyday, they're just not in the limelight.

Unfortunately, the police use the media to their advantage to smear our image as well. The media is always ready for a breaking story involving murder, drugs and mayhem, and those stories are usually highlighted because they draw more attention and more awareness when the defendant is Black. The police need to always show the reasons why they harass Black men and why they have to use violence when dealing with Black people. The media plays right into their hands by helping to create that image. The same crimes committed by black people that are being scrutinized by the media are being committed by white people less the exposure. Black people account for less of the crime committed in this country every year, but their image is portrayed a thousand times more in the media. And we are more likely to be given harsher sentences and sent to jail. So perceptions win in this case. Will that ever change? Only time will tell. Can Obama change that, too? I sure hope so. Our image needs reconstructive surgery and I sure hope he's the perfect surgeon for the job.

As much time as the media spends writing about crimes that Black people are involved in, it would be a great service to society if they spent half as much time highlighting some of the positive events that take place in the community as well. The Harlem Book Fair, which has become a staple in the Harlem section of Manhattan, has to pull teeth to get any kind of coverage by the mainstream media in New York City. Positive events where Black authors and readers should be encouraged just don't cut it, because the media's ink space or airtime is only good for the negative stories about us. Harlem is not the only place where events like these take place. It's the same story in Boston with the Harlem Book Fair Roxbury and the Boston Book Bazaar and pretty much all the other cities that hold book fairs every year. No balance to our image whatsoever is being depicted on paper or television by the media. Occasionally, we might get an honorable one-liner mention. What happens to fair and balanced reporting? It is a wonder that the media has not taken notice on the sudden interest in black literature by our youth.

31

Dispelling the Myths

The fact that the media most of the time portrays Black folks in a negative light continues to perpetuate the myth that Black people are violent, lazy, and want something for nothing. Let's take a look at the first myth: violent. Someone was smart enough to create a campaign to have the whole world believe that we're violent savages. The propaganda used to spread this across the globe has been very effective. We can look at a number of countries on the African continent and believe that to be the case. We don't have to look that far to see that's also what's going on in Haiti. Who's really behind all this violence that is going on? Are those Black people producing arms? Last time I checked, most guns were fabricated in the United States and exported to these foreign countries, but we're not going to concern ourselves with a global epidemic. We're going to try to focus on the problem locally in the United States. My research has shown that the United States government has been the culprit behind most of the civil and other ethnic wars as well as coup d'etats around the world. That's a whole new book that we won't get into right now.

However, what I will visit is the history of violence in this country. Under the chapter titled "Cruelty," I invite readers to take a closer look at how some of us have become the demons that society has portrayed us to be. Most intelligent people understand that the root of violence started with deceiving the Indians and the enslavement of Black people in this country. We'll have to wait for my perspective on that later, because I need to dispel a few myths right now.

I have visited many hoods in my life and not once have I been to one where there was a gun manufacturer or a factory producing guns. Given all the killings that take place in the Black neighborhood, it would have been nice to see that a few families are fed through the labor of gun production in the hood. After all, gunfire is the number one cause of death in the hood and we might as well reap some benefits from it, right? Wrong!! We're exploited at every angle of the game. It would have been easier for me to understand why so many Black men are murdered every year by a gun if members of our families worked for the manufacturer and smuggled the guns out illegally, but I've never met a Black person in the hood who worked for Smith and Wesson. However, I'm baffled by how many guns are found in the hood everyday. We get killed by guns even when we're not in contact with a gun. I'll let the police think about that one and I'll have my own explanation later.

Somehow, someway there seems to be a gun chief in the hood. He's able to bring thousands of guns through the hood without ever being noticed. The amount of guns that are available in the hoods across America is equivalent to the arms trade between the United States and Iraq. We provided Saddam with a lot of guns to keep those goons in check, but look at what's happening now. Well, the gun problem in the hood has not reached that proportion regionally, but collectively, we have more people dying of gun violence in the hood than Iraq. I'm starting to sound like a statistician, but I'm not. This is public information available on the internet. There are reports of Iraqis killing each other everyday just like the Blacks do in the United States, but there seems to always be the same culprit, a gang of some sort. In Iraq, that gang is under the command of Bush, but in the hood the culprit is a unified police force made up of all kinds of people. I can't fault the soldiers in Iraq because they never intended to be part of a gang. However, since their leader has a gangster mentality, they're forced to act like gang members, fighting for no reason at all and they have to obey the command of their chief.

Many of the soldiers joined the army to provide a better life for themselves and their families without ever thinking that they'd one day be risking their lives based on fabricated intelligence by the United States government. If any gang member on the street acted like Bush, he would probably be tried and subjected to life in prison or death for the mass murders of innocent people. Somehow though, Bush manages to evade impeachment and continues to fight a war with no means or end. This mentality trickles down to the state and local level and that is why this circle of violence will never cease. The government can't even admit when they're wrong, so what do we expect the police department to do when they're wrong? They have to fabricate stories as well as evidence and someone always has to take the blame and unfortunately in America the Black man has always been an easy target.

Being a target also leads me into the second myth that people tend to believe about Black folks because it's perpetuated on television twenty-four hours a day. People have this notion that we're lazy and I honestly wondered who had the balls to even come up with that one. First of all, lazy were those people who stood by and watched as black people worked and developed their lands for free without as much as a small compensation. Laziness is the fear that if a black man is allowed to obtain an education he might become smarter and a threat to an equal and fair chance in society.

How can they call us lazy when their history demonstrates that they've always been looking for the easy way? Wall Street is the biggest legitimate front for this. People lose the shirts on their backs everyday because of their laziness. No one is immune from the belly of the beast. CEO's are finally going to jail for stealing after so many years. The rich continues to get rich off the backs of poor people while the poor continues to struggle without even a chance of leverage. No, we're not lazy, our forefathers have broken their backs for many years and since you can't find a legitimate way to continue the enslavement of black people, we're referred to as lazy.

Lazy is taking advantage of talented young men to fill your stadiums while reaping the benefits of billions of dollars for your spectator sports without providing a conduit to help these young men with their life skills. Lazy is putting an age limit on black athletes because they have dominated basketball and you want to keep them from earning a living. However, it was okay for a 9-year old slave to be out in the cotton field to fill your pockets. Did you not care abut the black men's education then? The rules change very quickly when Black people dominate any industry in this country. Even a few Black people have been sold on the idea that these kids need to be exploited in college for a couple of years before they should be able to earn a living. How can you tell an 18-year old that he has to wait until he's 19 years old to start earning a living, however, it's okay for a 16-year-old white boys to turn professional in tennis, and also be drafted by Major League Baseball and the National Hockey League straight from high school? Are we really lazy? Or are they trying to take advantage of us? Which is it? Let's get real here.

A man can vote at eighteen, he can be tried as an adult, he can get married, but he doesn't have the right to get a professional job in the NBA or NFL? However, if he wants to go to McDonald's to get a full-time job, it's perfectly okay. That sounds ludicrous to me. Then again, I should know better. The institutions have the right to capitalize on the talents of these young men while their families have their backs against the wall in some project somewhere with very little resources. Instead of allowing these young men the opportunity to earn a living as soon as they are able to, these corporate thieves rather subject their families to a longer period of suffering, poverty, violence and even the possibility of death. These athletes sometimes have to go home to visit their families in the projects, and not everybody is always happy to see them.

32

White Justice Vs Black Justice

It's kind of interesting how white people and black people view things so differently. Most of the time, a lot of white people don't even realize that they're reinforcing a behavior that's detrimental to society as a whole. I can cite many cases where white people see certain actions by police officers as justified even with videotape footage as evidence. The Rodney King case is the easiest example that I can use to show how divided we are in opinions. Rodney King is a fool and we all know that, but he didn't deserve that Jim Crow beating he received at the hands of those police officers in Los Angeles. I always wondered what kind of lens the jurors were looking through to decide that the cops hadn't gone overboard with their excessive beating of Rodney King. Since I don't have blue or green eyes, I will never know what they see. What I do know is that every time a police officer is able to get away with such destructive behavior it only reinforces the fact that this country is more racist than ever. Not only that, it also confirms the fact that cops are allowed to get away with murder as long as their crime is committed against an alleged Black offender.

Initially, I had planned to cite different cases to make my points to support my arguments, but I found the task tedious because the information was endless and I did not know where to begin or end. Instead, I have decided to talk about situations and events that have been publicized on television in this chapter hoping that people will come to their own conclusions based on my presentation and the evidence of these well-known cases. My father always thought I was going to be the first lawyer in the family because I always present the best arguments during family gatherings. I can argue my ass off at the dinner table, but I found out that in court the judge has the right to tell me to shut up or be locked up. I basically had no voice. That actually happened to me once when I had to defend myself against a police officer in court for arresting me unjustly. The judge would not give me a chance to speak, so I just accepted whatever decision he made.

Since civil lawsuits are a big part of American life, I want to encourage my brothers and sisters who have been wronged by cops to personally sue them. White people have perfected the art of suing and it's about time that black people start exercising their rights to sue. If the criminal justice system won't prosecute them, render them penniless in civil court. It's been done to O.J and many others, so why not the cops. They have assets, too. Maybe these officers will straighten out their act if they know that they will be personally bankrupt because of their illegal actions.

New York City and Los Angeles are the most famous cities known for violating the civil rights of Black people during arrests. The videotape footage of police officers in California slamming a kid who was handcuffed on the hood of their patrol car wasn't enough to warrant an immediate dismissal from the police force. An investigation had to be done first and black people everywhere wondered "what's to investigate?" The proof was on camera. Sometimes, the judges are worse than the jurors. I'd like to wear their eyeglasses even if only for one day. They sometimes seem to interpret the law according to their own assessment and personal judgment, not what is legally binding in the law books. Talking about books, I wonder sometimes if the white men that wrote these books specifically created certain laws to punish the Black man exclusively. It just seems that way most of the time. The oppression that we go through in our daily lives is unbearable, degrading and cruel. Immigrants from every country come to America and the first thing they learn is that Black people are criminals. After most of these immigrants have become American citizens and are called to jury duty, their decisions are usually based on the prejudice that Black people are always guilty of crimes because we're perceived as criminals.

No black person is exempt from the presumption of guilt for a criminal activity. "Of course, Dr. Tyrone Brown surprised us with his action, but he's black and the criminal elements never left him even though he worked hard to become a doctor. He's guilty." That was just my example of a white colleague who found out a black doctor he's worked with for many years has allegedly committed a crime. This situation is as real as they come for Black men no matter what their status is in this country.

The law states that people are supposed to be tried by a jury of their peers, right? Why is it that in most black cases the jurors selected most of the time are white? Doesn't the word peer mean one who has equal standing with another? At least, that's the definition according to The American Heritage Dictionary. If that's the case, how can any white juror from a white suburb stand equally with any black person from the black community? Shouldn't our peers come from communities similar to ours? Every now and then we might find one or two black jurors, but the other ten usually have no idea about the burden of being black in this country. Being black is a burden for many of us because too many racists exist in this society. We can read one or two things in the way that the American jury is selected; one is that they are subliminally saying that black people aren't capable of making fair and right decisions or they're telling us that only the opinions of white people are valid.

It's always going to be easier for white people to get the kind of justice that is usually an injustice to us when it is a crime committed by a white person against a black person. The word "peer" is always relevant when the defendant is white because the jurors are usually mostly white. However, we very seldom find people from the hood as part of the jury when a black person is on trial for a crime against a white person. Why is that? If I live the hood, I would expect that my peers would be living in the hood as well.

O. J Simpson's situation was a little different, but the prosecutor failed to use the close identity that O.J. shared with his white neighbors to his advantage during the jury selection in his trial. There were just too many black people on O.J.'s jury. Half of these people couldn't even identify with O.J. and in the end, they were confused and could only render a "not guilty" verdict. Had the prosecutor used a white jury, which would have been closely identified as O.J's peers, the decision in that case could have very well been a different one. It's no secret that O.J. was the whitest black man in America behind Michael Jackson. His friends were mostly white and the women that he dated after he became a star was one hundred percent white. How could anybody in their right mind think that O.J.'s peers would be black? The wrong jury was selected and the wrong decision rendered. White people are still steaming over that decision. Just imagine how black people have felt for the last hundred years.

O.J Simpson was found innocent in court by a jury of his supposed peers, but white people will never let him forget that he got away with murder. I'm not an O.J Simpson fan, and never have been more than an admirer of his great accomplishments on the field, but I find it disturbing that Robert Blake's case has totally died down in the media while people still want revenge against O. J. The justice system is fair as long as white people agree with the court's decision. The court of public opinion will always linger.

Most white people were mad that a lot of Black folks appeared to have been celebrating O.J's innocent verdict for the murder of his wife, Nicole Simpson. What these white people don't realize is that most of these people are just like me, they don't give a damn about O.J. All they saw was that a black man finally found justice in the justice system in America. He used to run across airports hawking more products than Mr. America himself. The Black community never identified with O.J, but they embraced his situation because of the long oppressed situation they have suffered at the hands of the courts in America. People like Tiger Woods, Michael Jackson and O. J Simpson usually get rude awakenings from white America when they find themselves in a bind that involves the integrity of white folks. Because they're made to feel accepted due to their talents when they're on top, some of these famous athletes and entertainers feel that they're personally loved. Their spouse and circle of friends are always different from their own personal background. Statements like "I can't relate to Black women" is often heard coming out of these men's mouths. I don't have a problem with a man dating out of his race for love, but I don't want to hear that you can't relate to your own kind, because you are now a rich black man.

The mistakes are often repeated and the white trophy on their arms is usually alright until something negative happens in their relationship and then they're ostracized by white people. Black people always welcome them back with open arms and would even fight for them because that's the type of people we are. We are a forgiving people and we always accept the return of our prodigal sons. It's usually the men often times that turn their backs on the Black women that look like the woman who gave life to them. These men must also realize that no matter how far removed they are from the black world, when it comes down to it, they are still black and their children will be black no matter how fair in complexion they come out. We should respect and cherish our black women. They are your mothers, sisters, cousins, aunties and sometimes best friends.

It's not just the black men who shun black women after they have reached the pinnacle of success, there occasionally might be sisters with hang-ups about back men as well. The difference between the sisters and the successful brothers is that the sisters are usually in search of happiness and after giving a few brothers a few tries, they usually go the other way to find what completes them. I once saw an interview where Tiger referred to himself as Cablasian and I hope that he never finds himself in a courtroom looking for Cablasian justice, because as stated on his birth certificate, he'll only discover African- American justice at the hand of a white judge or jury depending on the crime. I'm not saying that Tiger will ever commit any type of crime, but he's a celebrity and we all have a bad day every now and then. However, his days are scrutinized more than regular folks because he's a rich black man with a white wife.

I must also point out to those black men and women who claim that because they are successful, they have a harder time meeting black mates that are comparable to them in status and wealth that a white waitress or a nanny is also not comparable to them in status or wealth. Maybe before they use that excuse they should really reconsider who it is that they want to marry. The waitress who serves you at your favorite restaurant certainly can't be better than the sister who worked hard for four years to earn a Bachelor's Degree and an additional three years to earn a Jurist Doctorate, or not even the sister who spent four years to earn her Bachelors in Nursing. I won't even mention the sisters who worked hard to become Psychologists, MBA's and Medical doctors. Some of them have ten times the qualifications to be a wife. I find it hard to believe that these women aren't available to rich athletes. I'm either the luckiest guy on the planet or my swagger just has all these women swarming around me. And to the sisters, I truly understand your plights because too many of our brothers are locked up or just aren't doing as well as some of you. However, marrying a white man who's twenty years your elder is not exactly marrying up either. Unless you consider a lifetime of Viagra investment is worth your happiness.

Personally, I find these excuses from both groups to be asinine. If a person chooses to marry white for happiness, I'm all for it, but don't use negative stereotypes about people from your own race as the scapegoat for your personal choices.

My question is, and always will be, how can anybody else respect our heritage if we don't respect it ourselves? Most black people are pushed to say they're mixed with something and even the darkest black person would claim the diluted European blood from many generations ago to feel worthy. Unfortunately, the judges and the white jurors never care about their white ancestors in the courtroom. All they see is what's in front of them and the complexion usually never matter because black is black.

Justice to some black folks is when a black celebrity beats a case in court sometimes. It's the only time they ever see a black person get off after being charged with a crime. Celebrity trials are highly publicized and some are televised. Black people hold on to that hope personally because they know of so many people that have been victimized by the system unjustly. It's almost like the first time Tiger won at Augusta. We were all proud because we had been denied access to that course for so long and out of nowhere this

"Cablasian" kid who looks black to us, beat all the white men that ever played the game. We cheered for Tiger because he was our justice on the day he beat those white men. Anything that happens the first time for any black person is a form of personal justice to us. Jackie Robinson broke the color barrier and we saw it as justice. When Hank Aaron broke Babe Ruth's record, it was justice. Barry Bonds stomping his way to many baseball records will be justice to many of us. When we can't find justice in the courtroom, we will accept it from any where else.

A perfect example of injustice to black people, but is apparently justice to a white judge in Paris, Texas is the case of Shaquanda Cotton. In Paris, Texas, Judge Chuck Superville who ordered probation as a form of punishment for a 14-year-old white teenager who burned down her family home felt a different kind of justice needed to be applied when the case of Shaquanda Cotton, a black 15-year-old was brought before him. In the case of Shaquanda Cotton, Judge Superville, who's white, decided to sentence the fifteen year-old Cotton to seven years in prison for allegedly shoving a hall monitor at her high school, not a teacher, but a hall monitor.

Shaquanda who had never been in trouble had no prior arrest record, and the 58-year-old white teacher's aide was not hurt during the incident, according to published reports. Paris is a small town of 26,000 residents in northeast Texas. The obvious racist Lamar county judge wanted to teach the black teenager a lesson his own way, not according to the law books. The conviction was for "assault on a public servant." Shaquanda Cotton is to remain in prison until she turns twenty-one years old. To add insult to injury, the officials at the Texas Youth Commission declined to provide access to the case to the media, citing Texas law. "State law forbids us from acknowledging whether we have any youths in our system, despite the fifty million issues of print that's been run," according to Jim Hurley, a spokesperson for the Texas Youth Commission. "We'd have to break the law to talk about it." But it was okay for us to find out through the courts that this young lady had been unjustly sentenced. The imbalance in justice is definitely prominent in this case and this judge should be removed from the bench, and the case thrown out of court.

The case is currently under investigation by the U.S Department of Education while this young woman sits in jail because of what political activist has referred to as an egregious miscarriage of justice in a town with a long history of civil rights abuses. I'm not as politically correct as Dr. Howard Anderson, the president of the NAACP Branch in San Antonio. I call a spade a spade and the judge is a plain racist. In the same town, a white man was sentenced to probation for killing a 54-year-old black woman and her grandson with his truck. The racist judge in that case ordered the man to send a Christmas card every year to the family to remind them of their pain. Totally disrespectful!

According to attorney Gary Bledsoe who heads the NAACP legal branch, Shaquanda was merely defending herself against an attacking teacher's aide. "All Shaquanda did was grab the aide to prevent a strike," Bledsoe said. Trying to keep black folks in their place has been the slogan in the courts in Paris, Texas. Intimidation and illegal tactics by police and judges are the norm. I have never been to Paris, Texas and I probably never will, but I can bet that they fought hard to prevent slavery from being abolished. According to local leaders, the town of Paris' efforts to keep blacks in their place is nothing new. Known as the site of the first highly publicized lynching of a Black man by a large racist white mob, Paris has a history of shame and bigotry. A fugitive by the name of Henry White was captured in Arkansas and brought to Paris, where, according to news accounts and published reports, he was tortured and burned alive on a train bed as more than ten thousand angry racist townsfolk cheered and jeered. Sometimes it seems like racism is so deeply embedded in these backward rednecks that they take pleasure in torturing people like it's a sport.

Times may have changed but the same racist attitudes and views remain. Education is supposed to broaden the mind, but these back wood judges who attended schools in the south somehow remained true to their racist southern roots. It's a wonder that they even went to school at all. This situation is just another example of modern day lynching going on in Texas. Meanwhile, a teenager has wasted a year of her life behind bars while people take their time to investigate. That judge should be ordered to serve the same sentence for taking the law into his own hands. It's weird that these people think that black people are going to sit by and continue to accept this kind of injustice. There is a fine line between sanity and insanity and when push comes to shove, some people won't give a damn as long as injustice continues to be the way of life.

I don't know if there's room for another Martin Luther King. Even Dr. Martin Luther King himself, an extraordinary human being was growing tired to the maltreatment and injustice against his people. However, before he and Malcolm started to be on accord with each other, their assassination was ordered. Well, there'll be a lot more assassinations ordered if the federal government doesn't step in soon and say enough is enough.

According to published reports, Shaquanda's sentence has been extended while serving time because she refuses to admit guilt. Not only was the sentence unjust, she's also being coerced into admitting guilt to a crime that she didn't commit. It's another case of law enforcement injustice. Shaquanda was also singled out because she repeatedly accused the school district of racism on several occasions. Accusing a school district of racism is nothing new. My high school principal was the biggest racist I knew and my school district did nothing to remove him. Most of the people who work in most of the school districts in America know good and well that there's racism going on, they just don't feel the need to do anything about it because it doesn't affect them, only the black students.

Even though twelve documented complaints of racism have been filed against the school district in Paris, Texas in recent years, nothing has been done about it. District officials vehemently deny the charges. However, the U.S Department of Education investigating the case has asked the U.S Department of Justice to get involved. When author Kevin Heubush named Paris, Texas "Best Small Town in Texas," in his book, The New Rating Guide To Life In America's Small Cities, he must've been oblivious to the racism and only focused on white lifestyle during his research. Now it makes me wonder about the author's credibility as well. You cannot write a book about the best places to live and be bias about it. Hopefully, black people stayed away from that book.

After a letter drive and petition aimed at Judge Superville, Shaquanda Cotton was finally released from prison. Now she has the chance to regain the normalcy that are prevalent in a teenager's' life, such as watching television, homework and talking on the phone for endless hours with friends and family. Shaquanda is out of prison in part because of Howard Witt, the Chicago Tribune writer and the original author of the article about the injustice in the small town of Paris, Texas.

Unfortunately, Shaquanda's case is not isolated; there are many other cases similar to hers in many small towns in America. Countless black men have been exonerated from heinous crimes that they have never committed due in part to the innovation of DNA technology and the effort of selfless individuals who believe in the reason why they attended law school in the first place, to fight for justice. The attorneys from the NAACP and the ACLU are the reasons why some of the injustices in this country have been righted. Many black men have been placed on death row and taken from their families based on the testimonies of false witnesses created by police to "testilie" in order to get convictions.

I most cases, those who gave false testimonies to the court are never prosecuted for obstruction of justice and they get to live their lives without any interruptions. The compensation that these innocent people usually receive isn't worth the time they spend behind bars and the half-hearted apology by the governor. This flawed system has also taken many lives because corrupted police officers are respected until their corruption somehow surfaces through an investigation.

33

Our Own Contribution to the Maltreatment

Since "keepin' it real" has been the motto in the hood for the last few years, I guess I'm gonna have to keep it real with my readers. Sometimes, we have to take a hard look at ourselves to see whether or not we have contributed to our situation in this country. Dr. Martin Luther King, Malcolm X and many other civil rights activists are probably turning over in their graves because of our detrimental behaviors. It's easy to say that the cops are wrong when one of us is shot dead by them for no reason at all, but the perception on their part is that they have reasons to kill us. The minority few have made it okay for the majority to get abused.

There are many factors as to why they feel that way. One officer in particular from Boston explained to me that Black men are most likely to pack heat. I guess packing heat is another way to feel safe around their own people because black people are also too scared of each other. We show more fear towards each other than white people do sometimes. Brothers just don't trust each other for whatever reason and if we can't do that, how can we expect the police to trust us?

Black men talking about harming each other in the hood echoes like symphonies coming from the halls of the Wang Center in Boston, and it makes me sick. You can pick any hood at anytime and you bound to find a young brother talking about his frustrations with another brother, and most of the time the easiest solution to their problems appears to be the total demise of their fellow brothers. There's a huge problem of conflict resolution in the hood and no one has offered any solution for it. These young men are growing up thinking that violence is the only way to solve their problems and respect can only be obtained with a gun.

There are many mothers out there who have no idea where their sons are at night or what activities they're partaking in, but those same mothers have the loudest cries and can cry a river at the mention of their son's name in any kind of deadly altercation whether it's with the police or another individual. Their son was always innocent and posed no threat to anybody. Those mothers are the ones in denial and we need them to start taking the role of a parent and make sure that their 12-year-old sons are not standing on the corner at eleven o'clock at night wearing a hoodie looking for potential customers to sell drugs to. Let's keep it real here; we do have people in the black neighborhood destroying it with their drugs, prostitution and petty crimes. It's not by accident that a 12-year-old kid decides he wants to sell drugs. It's because of the lack of parental guidance and most of the time a good role model and parental supervision all together.

I'm tired of welfare and working mothers prioritizing the next pair of Michael Jordan for their sons. What kind of moral compass are we using when we're putting first the material need of a child ahead of his well-being and education? Another thing, we are allowing these kids a sense of entitlement. I understand that sometimes welfare or government assistance is necessary when a person needs a boost in their life, but please let's not take money intended to provide relief and spend it frivolously on unnecessary items that will only force a child to grow accustomed to something, that in reality, they can't truly afford. Let me make something very clear: I do not want to receive hate mail from the welfare mothers who are guilty of some of the things that I mentioned in this chapter. If you have time to write a hate mail to me, you should also have time to spend with your kid helping him/her with his/her homework. Also, the latest designer fashion and the need to make a child feel like he/she belongs shouldn't cloud our judgment against the basic necessities. A kid can only want something that he feels he's entitled to because a parent has made that kid feel that he should wear a certain kind of shoes or clothing. Entitlement is usually the nemesis of laziness.

We are raising far too many fatherless young men and women who feel that designer clothes, jewelry, a Mercedes and not their education is a priority. These are some of the reasons why they turn to drug dealing and other illegal activities by the time they feel that they're man enough to stand on their block and turn every possible neighbor that they've grown up with to a crackhead or a heroin addict. We need to take responsibility for ourselves in order for people to start looking at us differently and give us the respect that our forefathers fought so hard and degraded themselves for. It takes a strong man to stand up against racism and show resistance against violence. Honestly, I could not do it and that's one of the reasons why I want to make sure that Dr. Martin Luther King didn't die in vain.

It's not just the lack of parental guidance, but it's also the music that we listen to. How can a police officer respect a man who calls black women bitches and hoes? How can they look at a black man as a man when this black man thinks that he's a nigga? How can they possibly show us respect when we walk around with our pants sagging off our asses like we're in jail telling other convicts that we're ready for action? How can we get any respect when we walk around acting like going to jail is a badge of honor? How can we gain respect when we try to emulate prisoners by wearing prison uniforms and calling it a fashion statement? How can we get any respect at all when the number of black men going to jail is higher then the number going to college? How can we get respect from anybody when we think that it is corny for a black person to act smart or be smart? How can we obtain any respect when we think of black people who speak proper English as sell-outs? These should be rhetorical questions, but what good are they because some of us still need answers.

I can only try to elaborate and give what I feel are the proper answers to these questions, but that would only be speculation on my part. It's always easy to speculate how things could be for the next man when you're not wearing the next man's shoes. I don't really know why some of us do what we do, or why we act the way that we act, but what I do know is that we're still affected by slavery and some of the behaviors we display are also inherited. Most people would love to dismiss slavery as something of the past, but nothing can be further from the truth. Nothing has been done to deal with the after effect of slavery and many grandparents were ill prepared to raise children and that lack of preparation has been passed on from generation to generation. Black people have adopted everything negative from slavery and make it a part of their lives.

Chitterling is the worst part of the pig that any person in their right mind can eat, but some black folks have a love affair with pig intestines. The history of chitterlings is not even passed on to the new generation because of our love affair with it. The pig intestines were given to black folks during slavery as another way to degrade them. That's all they were allowed to eat from a whole pig. White folks used whips and other forms of corporal punishment to "discipline" their slaves for centuries. Unfortunately, black folks have adopted the bad ways of the master to discipline their children. Many of these former slaves were ill equipped for a lot of things, but nothing was done to help them assimilate into their new life. We try to take away the negative connotation out of everything that we have adopted from slavery, but when we finally able to obtain success from it, we struck down by a law preventing us from doing it.

The child abuse laws have prevented a lot of black parents from having a hold on their children. They knew no other way for a long time and the one "good way" they felt they knew to discipline their children has been taken away from them. What are they to do? There has been no restitution of any kind for slavery, we have been lied to about our forty acres and a mule and manipulated into thinking that we were less human for many years. And now the world wants to blame us for the way that we act? Too many of us have yet to overcome the pain inflicted by slavery. Some of the psychological affects are still relevant and some of us understand that slavery has taken a new shape and form in the prison system.

Arm has been the American way for a long time, and most of us grow up believing that arming ourselves will instill fear, give us confidence and make us look tough, and the myth in the hood is that those three things equal respect. We preach nonviolence as a country all the time, but the American government often resorts to violence to sort their own problems. Assassins are hired to kill leaders overseas who disagree with our policies. Arms are usually used against nations to instill fear. America continues to develop Nuclear and other forms of destructive arms in case our livelihood is threatened. So, how are these kids supposed to change their mentality?

34

Paralysis by Analysis

One of the most detrimental things that Black people can do to each other is using the N word like it's a term of endearment. Some people argue that it doesn't have the same meaning because they spell it N-I-G-G-A. However, the pronunciation is a little too close for comfort and the connotation is definitely the same as if a racist in a white robe were saying it. It doesn't matter how the word is spelled, it still has the same meaning and it can never be endeared. We have to stop thinking that way about our brothers and sisters in order for the cops to change their way of thinking about us. Too many Black men think very little of their fellow Black men. Most of them won't hesitate to put a slug into another because of that "Just Another Nigga" mentality. Only we can allow ourselves to be thought of as "Niggas." Nobody is pushing it down our throats; we're voluntarily referring to each other as that. Some people have intellectually debated the worthless affect of the word when we use it toward one another, but it still carries a great amount of weight when it is spoken. White people are shocked when we call each other the N word and black people get pissed when white people call us the N word. What's the solution?

Some of us don't realize how easy it is to take away the value of a man by referring to him as a Nigga or Nigger. It is that ignorance and that lack of respect that make it so easy for us to kill each other for very little reason. The dots are subconsciously connected psychologically where respect is removed from the mind the minute we start thinking that this is "just another Nigga." We can all attach the word Nigger to someone whose life is worthless and that has been the historical context in which we have understood the word. That history has never gone away and it sometimes takes away responsibility when we think of someone as a Nigger. By no means, am I a psychologist, but I'm very analytical and from an analytical point of view, that word has completely paralyzed us.

I used to wonder sometimes why it's so easy for us to kill each other over dumb and stupid things, but we would never think about shooting a white person so easily because of the fear and respect that some of us have developed for white justice. First, let me clarify that no one should be shooting anybody, black or white. By reason of insanity or ignorance we seem to have fallen into a trap where we think less of ourselves because of something that took place more than five decades ago. It must be addressed.

We have established reasons that the cops can actually use as excuses for failing to investigate Black-on-Black crimes. If it is just a case of "another Nigga," why should the police department waste its resources on investigating another Nigga? Niggas aren't people, they're savages. We can fool ourselves to think that the way we think about ourselves don't influence the way other people perceive us, but we should know better. We are very responsible for the way that we're perceived by others. The media is only using the resources given to them to further demonstrate to the world that we are indeed savages who have accepted that role when we continue to refer to each other as Niggas.

Some people will say that this book is very contradictory in many ways, and perhaps it is. We live in a contradictory society where we preach peace, but aren't afraid to start a war for no reason. Contradiction has been the American way for a while now and I'm a product of this society. So, pardon me if I'm flaunting my American influence. Responsibility lies in our hands and we can't expect anyone else to change us.

35

Stop Snitching

Whoever the idiot was who started the "stop snitching" campaign must've been following the blueprint of the other idiots from the NYPD who refer to police officers who testify against them as snitches. The police departments around this country have managed to instill fear in their fellow officers who carry badges and guns just like they do, imagine what a defenseless resident can do when criminals are telling them to stop snitching? The street gangs and criminals have adopted many characteristics from the police department. The ways of doing business and the tormenting of those who go against the grain. I've pointed out many situations in this book where the NYPD acted like a street gang and we should not be surprised that these gangs are able to conduct business in the same manner.

Society has to wonder how this negative campaign for witnesses to keep from testifying and releasing information to the police against criminals better known as the "Stop Snitching" campaign has garnered so much publicity. Why are we, as a society, so prone to negativity? I plan on starting a campaign called "Get a College Education" this summer and I hope to see the same media reaction to it. People like Brian

Williams from NBC Nightly News, 60 Minutes from CBS, Anderson Cooper from CNN and many other major news magazine and outlets have found a way to reach those people who are involved in the "Stop Snitching" campaign for interviews. I'm baffled by the media attention this filthy campaign has garnered because it just reinforces the whole notion that the American Media is only interested in the negative goings-on of the black community.

These so called "spokespeople" being interviewed do not represent everyone in the hood. I have never met Cam'ron, how the hell can e be a spokesperson for me? Just because a person is in the spotlight it doesn't mean that he/she has earned the right to become the mouthpiece for everyone in a particular community. The media needs to learn this before airing their news stories. To separate facts from fiction, idiots and intellects are from two different spectrums of the world, however, the idiots are usually more entertaining to the masses because of the dumb things that they do or speak about. We're not all part of this idiocy going on and please learn how to make the distinction.

Some of us have had family members shot and killed by some of these idiots and to think for a moment that we wouldn't testify on behalf of our friends and family is ludicrous. Personally, I don't give a damn about anybody who wants to kill people in their neighborhood and community. If a trigger is pulled in front of me, I don't care if it's the cops or the hard gangster named Tyrone, I will be in court telling the judge about the idiot who pulled the trigger. Am I a snitch? Hell no! But someone is definitely a killer and they definitely would be going to jail based on my testimony. I would help put them right where they belong, in jail. We don't all condone criminal behaviors, not from the cops, not from our neighbors, and not from anybody. It's only the criminals who have problems talking to police because the bad cops and the criminals have developed relationships that have gone sour. We don't all buy into this negative crap that goes on in the hood and let's stop promoting it through the media.

36

It's a Cruel World

It's funny that some people are quick to associate the word cruel in the same sentence as black people, most of the time. I have heard it too many times and from too many people. Taking a close look at the history of cruelty in this country, it is obvious where it stemmed from. Our image has disintegrated to the point where "the defendant" has been able to turn the tables on the plaintiff using the best tactics of reversed psychology. Cruel is having people work hard labor for free so you reap the profits of their hard work. While black people experienced cruelty to the highest degree in this country, the media, government and the so called left wing have managed to rebuild their image and pass it on to us. Whipping a man for wanting his freedom is cruel, to sic dogs on innocent children and nonviolent Civil Rights marchers depict cruelty, keeping a man from earning a living because of the color of his skin is cruel and creating barriers that would prevent any human being from becoming the best that they can be is a form of cruelty. Cruel behavior had to be learned and unfortunately we have to take the blame for it.

It's not just police officers who have a reputation of being cruel, back in the sixties firefighters were all too happy to take part in inflicting pain on innocent people when they were ordered to use their fire hoses on the Civil Rights protesters. I have yet to see clip footage of one of them standing up to say that wasn't right. That's the society we breed and we're under this delusion that young black men are given just as much opportunity as their counterparts?

It was cruel to get a 400 years headstart on us and suddenly decide that we need to catch up. What happened to our forty acres and a mule? That sure would've given us a chance for equilibrium. The cheating, lying, and violence didn't start with us. It started with the founders of this country who were too lazy to cultivate their own lands or develop their cities to the point where this nation is now known as the wealthiest. Wealthy on whose back, though?

What's cruel is the government has denied these young men access to a fair education, but will allow them to set up shop in the ghetto to sell drugs for years before finally busting them. Look around and see who are the people most affected by drugs, lack of healthcare and education? This country currently seems to run on the penal system. Jails are being expanded and Black and Latino men are rounded up daily to fill them. It's the new way of enslavement, it's called cheap labor. Most people have no idea what goes on behind the walls of prison, but I won't give you the answer because you need to find out for yourselves. Your sons, brothers, fathers and uncles are locked up because their slave labor is needed.

What's cruel is sentencing a 14-year-old to seven years in prison for allegedly shoving a teacher's aide in Paris, Texas. Does the rest of the world know what's going with Black people in this country? Apartheid didn't end in Africa, it started in America. And it's taking a more cruel shape and form. Thousands of police officers are sworn in daily around the country to enforce these apartheid rules. Now, it's being masked a different way because we have Black and Latino police officers contributing to it. It's all about the new field Negro and the house Negro. This new house Negro is made to fear his own brothers and sisters because they are viewed as cruel and heartless.

How are they supposed to deal with cruel and heartless people on the job? They have to become cruel and heartless themselves. An officer can't expect a Black man to act civil when he's trained to believe that Black men are cruel, deadly and heartless. He is going to make sure he safeguards his life first then if he has to, he'll worry about the Black man and deal with the consequences later. Those are the sentiments echoed amongst the police officers that I interviewed for this book.

Cruel is having the ability to convince the whole world that a particular race of people can be treated with no dignity like savages. Everybody who comes to America learns the word Nigger within the first year, but not only that, they also learn to fear Niggers as well. Asians, Indians, Arabs, Europeans even South Americans come to America fearing their lives in the presence of African-American. To add to that, their own fellow Black West Indian brothers feel the same way about them sometimes, too. Slavery has been able to separate black people all over the world. I'm not one to buy into the Willie Lynch rhetoric, but how do you explain so many Black men hating each other so much?

The harshest forms of cruelty took place many years ago, unacknowledged by American society, though the barbaric ways that Black people were treated has been documented everywhere. However, it continues to be the root of all our problems because even though the barbaric ways are not as prevalent anymore, there are still other measures used today that should be considered cruel. It's out with the old and in with the new, but the sufferers remain the same. Well, that's not completely true, because added to the list of sufferers are our brown brothers from across the border. Institutional racism has been perfected over time and now they have quite a few people foolishly believe that America offers the same opportunities to Black and Latino people as it does with the other races.

37

A Separate State of Mind

While watching a special about the lack of African-American presence in the sport of baseball, I was appalled that the African-American players didn't consider their Latino brethren like David Ortiz, Sammy Sosa, Manny Ramirez and many others as their Black brothers despite the fact they all share the same complexion. It is very dangerous when we actually allow the white media to separate black people based on their country and not. Until a dark skinned player from the Dominican Republic or Cuba opens his mouth and his Spanish accent is detected, he's considered a black man. African-Americans aren't the only ones to adopt this mental illness sprung on them by society. The Afro-Latino community accepts this bullshit as well. I call it bullshit because I have to call a spade a spade once again. How can two people with the same African heritage feel that they're so different because of the languages that they speak?

This wedge between the different groups was created for a reason. Caribbean people living in America are often shunned from the African-American community in America. The school system in America is to blame because a lot of information about black and brown people from across the world who have contributed to this country's development and growth is kept out of the history books. To alleviate some of the existing problems that create the separate state of mind in this country amongst people of color, I did a little research of my own to try to empower all people of color and hopefully bring some unity to the different groups, even the light skinned and dark skinned African Americans and other blacks who continue to distinguish themselves based on their complexion.

The nature of Black American identity has been lost because historical facts have been kept from them. As African-Americans have been told historically, any person born in America who is of African ancestry or possesses African characteristics is considered African-American, however remote their ancestry is. That basically means the parents can be from Jamaica, Haiti, Barbados, Nigeria or any other black country and they would be considered African-American as long as they're born in the United States of America. African-Americans don't always see it that way. Many American born children to foreign parents often speak the native tongue of the parents, and that reason creates exclusion from the African-American community. Unless a Black man was born on American soil he's not to be considered African-American, but he's considered African-American even though his parents may be from the West Indies? That's something to think about.

Also added to the equation, is the one-drop rule, invented and imposed by some of America's white racists until the middle of the 20th century. It's no surprise that African- Americans turned this racist doctrine to their advantage as it relates to ethno-racial relations. The white racists' initial point of attack was to show the impurity of their race with the one drop rule. However, African-Americans took it as a badge of pride and inclusion. It significantly became to Blacks a glorious principle of inclusion that has created another division amongst Blacks, which white racists intended for it to be a means of exclusion. White looking Blacks found it absurd to be referred to as Blacks, because the one drop rule excluded them. But Blacks used the same rule to enlarge the Black population and its leadership with very light skinned people who have issues considering themselves Black in America and the West Indies. This issue created a different kind of separation amongst the Black population and the mulattoes (people of mixed heritage).

Though black identity has been distorted in this country, however, historically it was proven to be progressive early in the 19th century through the civil rights movement. Then Black leaders took more interest in black oppression around the world, not just America. Movements like the Pan-African movement and Black Nationalism gave strength to Black solidarity and pride. The Haitian revolution brought pride to blacks in America and the rest of the world as they were the first black republic and the only army to defeat the French army. And Black American missionaries played an important role in converting many Jamaicans and other West Indians to Christianity. Black Americans were also inspired and open to the idea of Black immigrants as it increased the black population in America. Those sentiments seem to be no longer amongst Black Americans, but that might be because of the lack of history on the background of some of America's greatest black achievers. The government has managed to turn many Black Americans against other Blacks who emigrated here from other countries. The vast difference in treatment and policies towards the Haitians and Cuban immigrants is valid proof of the racist attitudes still carried by this government against people of color.

W.E. B Dubois' father was Haitian, Jean Baptist Point Du Sable who discovered Chicago was also a Haitian merchant, James Weldon Johnson's mother was Bahamian and Sidney Poitier was also Bahamian. Marcus Garvey, who led one of the first mass movements of African-Americans, was Jamaican. Other leaders with West Indian backgrounds include Malcolm X, Stokely Carmichael, Shirley Chisholm, Minister Louis Farrakhan, Harry Belafonte and many more were all first or second generation immigrants. Prior to the notables mentioned above, West Indians played an instrumental role in New York City politics. The inclusiveness needed in the African-American community to bring solidarity is only absent because of the lack of information.

We'll continue to be divided and conquered as long as we continue to allow the differences in our cultural backgrounds to be a nuisance to our unity. Instead, we should embrace the commonalities, which most often is our skin color. The police or American bigots can care less about your heritage when you get caught in their line of fire. A great case and point can be the many different victims highlighted in this book. They were from all different backgrounds, but the common thing that they shared was their skin color. We need to wake up as a people and take charge of the direction in which we want to go.

The weird thing about the separate state of mind is that when Black men from any country are asked to check their race on any type of employment application or other government applications needed for data, they're usually given one choice, and that choice is usually Black. How can a black man with black skin consider himself to be only Latino? How did he inherit his black skin? Maybe one day we'll all be considered Black as do the white folks who don't differentiate between Irish, Polish French or Italians.

38

Identity Crisis

African-Americans seem to be suffering from the worse case of identity crisis known to man. Figuring out the reason for this crisis is the most troubling part. Young people no longer see their parents as role models because the crack epidemic of the eighties has taken away the dignity of many mothers and fathers. The crack babies are now in their late teens and early twenties and they have taken on a new personality of their own. The long term affect of crack and other drugs on these kids and their families is alarming.

New York City's black population has seen the most devastated affect of crack. This devastation is not only physical; it has ruined the fabric of what used to be called a community. With crack, came all the other maladies, such as thievery, prostitution, murder and the evaporating trust of the community. Steel bars on doors and windows became an essential part of daily life. Crack addicts are feared because the need to feed their addiction leaves very little room for trust. Mothers and fathers suddenly have to grow a third eye around their own children who have fallen victim to this epidemic. Everything and anything is valuable to a crack head. The family living room is no longer a place where families gather to watch television, it becomes the guarded part of the house where crack addicted kinfolks are watched because of their inability to cope with their drug habit and have to resort to stealing from their own mother and father to support their vice. The VCR suddenly has to be under lock and key and the quarrels about missing items and money adds to the already existing tension.

Former faithfully religious homes are turned upside down and no one but God seems to have the proper answer to the problems. Pastors understand that these families are vulnerable, and their dedication to the Lord has never wavered, so they play on their vulnerability sometimes. Most of the time, the church avoids the subject of drug addiction altogether. The pastor usually reinforces prayer as the only answer. No type of drug counseling is set up at the church to help these people, but their ten percent tithe contribution from the congregation is reminded every Sunday. The Grandparents have to play the role of parents for the welfare of their grandchildren. Grandchildren are calling their grandparents mom and dad while their grandparents help them understand that their other mother or other father will soon be coming back to help raise them. Confusion and chaos lead these kids to look to the street and television for guidance. Father figures and other role models are sought on BET and MTV became a surrogate mother to most ghetto children. The children are no longer allowed to go outside and play because the crack dealer is always recruiting and the grandparents don't have the time or energy to chase them away from their innocent little ones.

Some family members have to come to grip with the reality that their crack addicted kin have to be let go because of the threat and danger they pose to the family as a unit. They grow comfortable with the idea that death or an announcement of death on behalf of their crack addicted family member is lurking. Keeping the offspring of those addicts safe becomes a priority, but they usually lack the strength and energy to keep on top of the young. Money is short and the retirement checks are not enough to take care of the grandchildren. Food is now limited and the grandchildren are being ridiculed in school because grandma can't afford to buy them the latest brand name sneaker. The ripple affect starts to take form and sooner rather than later, the 12-year-old grandson finds himself on the street corner pushing drugs for that coward dealer who understands that the law can't put away a minor if caught. He capitalizes on this as well. Everybody gets used and abused by those closest to them because that seems to be the new way of the hood.

Now we have young boys feeling like they're men. They're making more money than their caring grandparents ever made. Their attitudes change and suddenly grandma starts to lose her footing in her own home because little man thinks he's big man because he can help pay the bills now. The booming sound of Hip Hop music lingering somewhere near becomes the voice of reason for these young men. Studio gangsters reinforce the street attitude. Getting paper and living large is what it's all about. Their given name at birth no longer suits them, there's no fear factor attached to anything. The old gangsters from the twenties and even some modern day and fictitious ones are now adopted. Most of the Hip Hop world conforms to this identity crisis as well, so it's okay for the corner dealer to identify himself as Corleone, Capone or some of the well-known names of former drug dealers who appear in every rap song, serving life sentences behind bars. The most famous ones, however, are John Gotti and the famous Hollywood fictitious character, Tony Montana from Scarface. Every little hustler on the street is now known by the name of a famous gangster just like their rapping role models. The other well-known gangsters, such as Escobar, Frank White and others whose lives were short because of the career path chosen, are now the epitome of success for young Black and Latino men. Completely ignorant to the fact that their lives will also be short lived because of that familiar path, these kids create a façade that makes them feel "hard" with utter disregard for another man's life.

This identity crisis is destroying our neighborhood and it just gives more ammunition to the cops to rid society of some of us. It's not fair to me and it's not fair to the Black men who wake up every morning to go punch the clock to help support their families. These men are left in the shadows and sometimes become victims of circumstances just because of the color of their skin. These working men's lives are at risk on both ends. They have to protect themselves and their children from both the drug dealers and the rogue cops. And a confrontation with either can lead to their demise. I hope we turn a new leaf very soon because the essence of respect and family are slowly leaving the hood, and indeed we are headed for destruction.

The big corporations have complete disregard for the working families. And the new millionaire athletes, even the ones who grew up with hardly any luxury in their homes, forget their humble beginnings. Signing their names on the dotted lines to endorse one hundred and fifty dollar sneakers is the trendy selfish thing to do. The young kids in the projects who feel that their identity is tied to an expensive sneaker will do almost anything to get their hands on those sneakers, risking their freedom for them or even take another person's life. Honorable athletes like Stephon Marbury and Ben Wallace who understand the plight of the poor family are frowned up for their effort in offering a more affordable sneaker of equal quality for these kids.

Gucci, Prada, Fendi, Manolo Blahnik, Versace and many other designers have become the staple of fashion for the hood even though these designers have no idea what the hood looks like. We can't blame them because they did not create this phenomenon. Materialism has been our identity for the last decade and the only people suffering from this are the kids whose parents are struggling to put food on the table everyday. It's easy to say that the parents are responsible to instill value in their children, but other children aren't taught not to be cruel to others. I wore cheap sneakers when I was kid and many of my classmates made fun of me. However, the weird thing about the people making fun of me was that most of them lived in the projects while I lived in a home owned by my striving, immigrant middleclass parents who clearly understood the way of the beast. We have a bad case of screwed up priorities that screws up our identities in the worse way.

The images, personalities and characteristics of pimps are now imitated. It has now become fashionable to be known as a pimp. Some rappers are even naming beverages after them. Our children seem to be getting screwed and anything and everything is being thrown their way by those who are from our community to victimize them even more. These images can be found online and on their favorite music television stations like BET, MTV and VH1. Shows like "Flavor Of Love and I Lone New York" have depicted the buffoonery portrayals that our forefathers have fought so hard to erase. These images are confusing to the youth because these people are being rewarded handsomely for their disturbed behaviors.

39

Oppressing Ourselves

Just imagine if we all woke up tomorrow and decided that we were going to collectively make Dr. Martin Luther King proud? The best way to honor him would be to show him that those cops who mistreated him without cause and those who threw rocks at him and hit him for no reason are eating their words and actions because we have indeed overcome. Imagine that? Imagine that illegal hustling no longer had to be a way of life. We're too intelligent as a people to allow ourselves to be controlled by our situations. We have limited resources and opportunities, and that is true, but what about those of us who have created opportunities with those limited resources that are available to us? Are we a people full of excuses?

Lately, it seems like we have opened so many doors and created so many opportunities for ourselves through Hip Hop and sports, but we don't know how to characterize everything in a positive way. Self-destruction has been the path leading to our demise and it can only be defined as a new way of self-oppression. We're oppressing ourselves and depriving ourselves the luxury of being respected and appreciated for our talent and as people.

All the money we have earned and talent we have exhibited and shared with this world has been defeating to our image. There's no more humility and self-respect left in the young Black generation anymore, it seems. I don't mean to generalize because there are plenty of young people holding their end of the bargain, but their efforts are overshadowed by those who have endless exposure in the media. It's so easy for me to make generalization about us as a people because we have over the years grown accustomed to it. The media doesn't want to portray the regular young black men who are striving and working hard to get their college degrees. They're not interested in the Black men who take on the responsibility to provide for their families. They don't car about the ones who go back to their communities to make a difference in other people's lives. They only care about the young men whose only concern is the total destruction of the black image. That's what the media seeks and the more they ask for it, the more we seem to give it to them.

Those young men working hard to climb the American corporate ladder face many obstacles due to the increased negative portrayal of our young black men in the entertainment industry and the six o'clock news. Most people have a hard time with our individuality because it gives justifications to their prejudice. That in turn, shuts the door on many of us who never dream of becoming entertainers. Shows like MTV Cribs only add fuel to the fire when the excessive lifestyle of these young black men is revealed to the public. Being a braggart is the new way to define manhood. While many athletes and rappers are quick to brag about the many cars, sneakers and chains they have and the size of their homes, they very seldom talk about what they do to help those they left behind in the community that helped them with their success.

Creating and formulating a plan for the studio gangster has been the toughest blow yet. I can sympathize with these young men because it's hard to walk away from millions of dollars. That opportunity only comes knocking once in a lifetime and if they have to sell their souls to the devils for that BMW or Mercedes Benz with twenty four inch rims, so be it. So many murders have been committed on records and so many drug cartels have openly been created, it's surprising that the FBI aren't rounding these young men by the thousands everyday. Murder, drug and mayhem have been the way of life for many rappers on wax without realizing the long lasting affect to their image and the detriment to the minds of the young and impressionable in our community.

It's hard to listen to Hip Hop without the reference of guns, drugs, bitches, hos, and money. Most rappers openly admit to carrying even bazookas in their songs. Is it entertaining? Maybe, but to a 12-year-old it might be reality. The record labels are one hundred percent behind these types of destructive lyrics. As a matter of fact, they encourage it. Being a gangster is a prerequisite to a recording contract even if a person has to make it up. The record executives don't care about the repercussions of these ill lyrics blasting in the ears our youths in the community because most often they are white and live in suburbia while the listeners are black and stuck in a world where they sometimes believe that they have to live up to these lyrics. Most often times, even the rappers themselves share their abode with their exec neighbors in suburbia while corrupting the hood with the negative figments of their imagination.

It is those lyrics that the police feel gives them the right to shoot first and ask questions later when they are dealing with young black men. We're creating a situation where even the most educated black men are at risk of losing their lives because of the image that we have allowed ourselves to fall victim to because of a few artists in the Hip Hop industry. The latest craze added to our negative image is the badge of honor associated with surviving gunshot victims. A criminal record is no longer impressive in the community anymore, now a person had to have been shot to be respected.

Music is not the only instrument being used to destroy the black community. Now, we also have "Urban Literature" where every story is glorifying the lifestyles of drug dealers, pimps and hustlers. The N-word is usually found at the end of every sentence and Bitches and hos make up most of the characters. Too many people seem to have something negative to write as a form of literature to our youth. This path of destruction is adopted at every turn and only the consumer can change this pattern of behavior. We must take a stand and tell everyone, writers, rappers, and athletes that they will be held to higher standards. And maybe only then will we start to see positive changes coming from those who try to exploit the ignorance of the community.

The Most Dangerous Gang in America: The NYPD

It is very oppressive when a young black man is not given respect when he's a college graduate, but is adored and respected the day that he walks out from a jail cell or from a hospital after being shot. Civility is almost nonexistent with these young men and they are being taught to be that way. Police officers are faced with the task of showing these young men that a bullet begets a bullet, but most of the time it's all braggadocio because there's usually no truth behind their lyrics. Publicity stunts for "street cred," usually end up being costly for these young men who managed to escape the belly of the beast. Unfortunately, most of them have to adhere to an image fabricated by executives to exploit them.

While Hip Hop can be credited for many positive changes in our culture, it also has contributed to many of the negative stereotypes towards black people. It is true that Hip Hop has crossed cultural lines, but I wouldn't attribute today's Hip Hop to that accomplishment. Long before there was 50 Cents, Jay Z or any of the well-known modern day rappers, Groups like Public Enemy, De La Soul, X Clan, Boogie Down Productions and LL Cool J were filling up stadiums across the country in a positive way with both Black and White people. NWA never intended for their ghetto strive to be exploited on wax by some studio gangsters who feel that their image have to hard core in order for their voices to be heard. Hip Hop has long been the voice of the ghetto and an expression for change, but how can we change anything if all we want to talk about is killing one another, calling our women bitches and hos, being a drug dealer or doing drugs and the excessive lifestyle we throw in the faces of those who support us?

40

Cause and Affect

Many people don't understand what cause and affect means as it relate to situations, business, well-being and life in general. If we continue to create a cause to give the cops even a fraction of reasons to shoot at us, we'll continue to suffer the affects. We have to organize ourselves as a new generation to represent us in the best light possible when situations like Sean Bell's arise. We can't continue to allow these cops and their lawyers to go to court and justify their actions because of our poor daily behaviors.

We have to start believing in ourselves more in order for other people to believe in us. It's not an accident that some people are threatened by our mere presence. Just check out our history and you can see the reasons why we are threatening to many. Not too many people could've endured what we've endured as a race and still live to influence the whole world. They tried to break us, but we're not broken. They tried to pity us, but we're not pitiful. When we apply ourselves, there's absolutely nothing in the world that we can't do. We've managed to become doctors, lawyers, engineers, inventors, pioneers, scholars, astronauts, writers, teachers, actors, and so many other professions despite the fact that our forefathers were prohibited from getting a basic education. The cause for these accomplishments was our natural zeal to adapt and learn, and the affect is to take our rightful place in society. We are smart and intelligent people despite what they say about us.

What happened to our determination to succeed against all odds? Why did Jackie Robinson subject himself to the cruel racism of this world? Was it not to make the world a better place for us? Rosa Parks risked her own freedom to create a world that would allow us the dignity of a normal human being. The cause of their actions was for the future generation and the affect is supposed to be for us to be part of a better world. We're taking all their progress and we're regressing in the worse way possible. Jackie as I would like to affectionately refer to the legend without any disrespect, fought to open the doors for black athletes in baseball, but we have fewer African-Americans interested in baseball or playing for Major League Baseball. Rosa Parks fought for the right to sit in front of the bus, but we always walk directly o the back of the bus. It's almost as if we are conditioned to be a certain way.

The cause and affect of this can be attributed to slavery, but too many people before us knew that it wasn't right to be treated a certain way and they fought to change that. We can't, after so many years ago continue to allow ourselves to be affected by the maltreatment that our forefathers received. Something has got to give and we can't let what happened in the twenties, thirties, forties, fifties and even the sixties take a new form by allowing ourselves to be lynched in a new and improved way. We have to take responsibility for ourselves in order for us to change the system. We can make all the demands we want, but if we're not changing our ways our demands will continue to be ignored.

41

Black Women

Although most cases of documented abused by police are usually against Black and Latino men, lately there have been many new cases involving women as well. Some women have allowed themselves to be bamboozled into thinking that they are "down ass chicks," supporting the detrimental behaviors of some of these black men. Hip Hop lyrics are laced with confessions of women holding down their men and even packing heat for them when necessary. While most of it may be for entertainment purposes only, the cops treat it as reality and these women aren't spared the violence and brutality used against the men.

Black women have been fighting for respect for a long time now, and it's getting harder for them to get that respect. Hip Hop has not been helping their cause either. However, Hip Hop should not be blamed completely for what's going on with black women and the cops. Women should also take responsibility for their own behavior as it relates to the way they are viewed and treated by society.

I knew that Oprah couldn't wait for the opportunity to jump on the rappers and Hip Hop after Don Imus' idiotic comments about black women. With that said, I watched the show that she did called, "Townhall" and thought that balance needed to be added to the issue. First of all, I must add that Oprah has never been a proponent of Hi Hop or even young black men for that matter. I don't think I have ever watched one of her shows that helped deal with some of the crisis that black men are faced with. It's always easier to jump on the bandwagon and pass the blame to us for society's demise, but very seldom are proactive steps taken to help alleviate the problems.

Also, I want to make it clear that I'm completely against rappers calling women bitches and hos and bragging about killing their fellow black men and selling drugs to their own community. Now that I've established that, I want to point out how some of the black women contribute to the detrimental behavior exhibited by rappers.

One of the first things I notice when I go out to clubs is that women, not just black, but all women rush to the dance floor sometimes by the thousands when the following songs are being played: Bitch Betta Have My Money by DJ Quick (old School), Area Code (I got hos in different area codes) or Move Bitch by Ludacris, Money Cash, Money Cash Hos by Jay Z, Any song by Snoop Dogg, Shake That Ass Bitch And Let Me See What You Got by some southern rapper and all the other misogynistic songs that you can find by rappers get the dance floor packed. If that's the case, I don’t understand how rappers are expected to completely take on the responsibility of denigrating our Black women. The reaction of some of these women encourages the continuation of the trend sometimes.

It's very easy to blame rappers and hold them accountable because they're in the limelight, but who's supporting these rappers? Women like Karen Stephans AKA Superhead who wrote “Confessions of a Video Vixen” and Carmen Bryan who penned “It's No Secret,” make it almost glamorous to be a toy to these rappers. As a matter of fact, they made writing careers out of their experience in the Hip Hop world, and became wealthy as well, doing it. Furthermore, beside white people Black women are the number one consumers of Hip Hop music, more than black men. After a concert, most of these rappers are sleeping with their female groupies who allow themselves to be called and treated like hos.

Of course, I don’t condone any type of negative behaviors toward Black women, but rappers didn’t come up with the concept of degrading Black women on their own, there has always been someone there to help them push the envelop. Those people are the ones who capitalize the most on the negative movement spearheaded by the rappers who are in the frontline taking full and complete responsibility for this shame that they have brought on our people.

I think Black women need to take a long look at themselves and ask the question "Are we partly to blame for this?" We can blame the music execs for pushing this trash, but it is being accepted by our own. When will we wake up? The separate state of mind has also played a big role in this misogyny going on in Hip Hop. There's always a group of women who remove themselves from what's being said because they like believe that, "they're not talking about me." No special group of Black women is ever singled out, so the negative comments pertained to all black women. The minute the divisive state of mind come into play, they're losing half the battle. It's the same thing with the professional Black men who feel that they're immune from police brutality because they're not wearing saggy jeans down their ass and they're not "living in da hood." The cops don't give a damn about your profession or where you live; all they think about is that you're a possible threat to them because you're Black.

I grew up with Hip Hop and I can honestly say that lately, I've only been able to listen to a few Hip Hop artists. It is very sad that my daughter and I can't enjoy the same kind of music. The lyrics are usually laced with profanities and I have to protect my infant daughter's ears from this trash. Hip Hop started to lose its essence the minute it became a billion dollar industry. People like Grand Master Flash, Afrika Bambata, Public Enemy and KRS One couldn't make it in Hip Hop today because they had too much to say to society. Hip Hop has become a hustle and with every hustle the talent is usually diluted.

I say this to the ladies, if you want change, you have to assert yourselves and demand change. Don't allow someone to get away with something that offends you. The same way Don Imus was taken off the air, you can collectively stop these rappers from calling you hos and demand that the sponsors stop supporting these radio stations who play this crap that they now call music. I'm not saying that everyone in the rap industry need to be like Common and the Roots, but calling women out their names and making a mockery of all the hard work that our forefathers have done to remove the label "Nigger" from our identity shouldn't be a way to make a living.

The cops act like big brother, they're always watching. The more ammunition we give them, the more reasons they will have to make victims out of us. If we don't respect ourselves, they sure as hell aren't going to respect us. Stop being a down ass chick who's looking for a roughneck who cares nothing about you and only thinks of you as a ho and a bitch.

Think about it, if every woman swore off drug dealers and misogynists tomorrow, most men would be behaving accordingly. Men are doing the crap that they're doing most of the time to impress women. Women need to raise their standards so that the men can follow. It's no secret that Black women are already ahead of Black men in our community. Now, let's help them change their behavior as well, so that they can be good fathers, husbands, brothers, lovers and friends. I challenge people like Oprah to pay closer attention to the brothers. I challenge BET to challenge these brothers to earn the spotlight on their television station for being righteous. I challenge MTV to require these young brothers to be respectful and descent in order to earn airplay. Most of all, I challenge my brothers to stand up and say it's time for change.

The easiest thing for a brother can do is to go to jail. The police can always find a reason to throw you in jail, but they can't keep you from getting an education. We're too smart a people to allow this self-destruction to continue. Our sisters should not subject themselves to strip searches every time they want to visit brothers at the prison. Think about your wives, kids, and family before giving the next cop reasons to unload his revolver on you. Let's stop contributing to our demise in all aspects of our lives. We are fading as a group and only we can do something about it, no one else. Ladies, you simply have to demand change and do not compromise your value and integrity for the sake of money, men or popularity.

42

The Purpose

Most organizations are created with a purpose. Be it financial, nonprofit, legal, school, or what have you, there's always a purpose behind the idea of an organization. Not all organizations' purposes are righteous. A good example of this, are gangs. They really serve no purpose to most people, but somehow there's a group of neglected children out there that feel that a gang can give them a place of belonging. It's almost like acceptance into a family, but that acceptance usually comes with a price. Most gangs require their members to commit some kind of heinous crime to show allegiance. And most impressionable teenagers would go to any length to prove that they belong. That association usually has ripple affects because anybody they come in contact with is also at risk.

A person doesn't have to be a gang member to be guilty by association. If for some reason I'm hanging with my best friend who happens to belong to the North Side gang, and we end up running into members of the rival South Side gang, a confrontation might ensue and I might become a victim by association. Whether or not I'm a gang member won't make a difference because the South Side gang members see two people and one of them is the enemy, and they have no idea what my intent is. When the primate fear kicks in, I'm more likely to be a victim.

Even pimps serve a purpose despite what many people may think. Pimps prey on the young and dislocated. Most runaways end up turning tricks on the street because that option is usually created for them by an opportunist called a pimp. That pimp understands the psychological state of that child and he has mastered the art to the point where he can easily convince that child to sell her body and give him the money. The mind is a powerful tool that can be used to manipulate the impressionable. Most runaways usually runaway because of the lack of love in their household or in some cases it can be physical, sexual or psychological abuse. To that end, comes the search for love. A pimp can spot a victim a mile away and an experienced pimp would position himself as a savior who loves unconditionally and therefore sets up bait for his victims.

Teachers, however, serve a greater purpose than all, but not all teachers are purposeful. As a former teacher, I had colleagues who were passionate about their profession. They served in more than one capacity. Sometimes, they were the disciplinarian, the loving parent, the advisor, guidance counselor, friend, positive reinforcement, motivator and molder that molded the students into great people. But there were teachers who also didn't belong in the classroom. They were the instigators who provoked the students in the classroom by undermining their abilities. I've actually heard teachers refer to students as dumb. I was not surprised because a teacher once referred to me as dumb. I'm not one to let anything slide, so a negative teacher would get checked in my presence. A good intention can turn to bad at anytime depending on the approach taken. Most teachers are respected, but not all teachers deserve respect. Those people who attended public schools in the urban parts of the country understand exactly what I'm talking about. It's a well known fact in the public school systems across the country that a lot of teachers are working just to get a paycheck. The passion for the profession does not exist in all of them.

Life in general has a purpose, but what we choose to do with it is up to us. I truly believe that the police departments across the country serve a purpose. However, not all police officers are purposeful. There are so many great purposes for having a good police force, but I'm only going to touch upon a few right now. For instance, sometimes we leave our house and have no idea if we'll ever make it back home in one piece. It could be that maniac with a Nine Millimeter Glock who decides that his life serves no purpose and wants to take away your life. Armed with a handgun and you're at his mercy, he can easily control your destiny. It is now up to him whether or not you make it back home to your family, unless a purposeful officer is called to the rescue. I don't know much about the tactical aspect of their training, but I do know that it sometimes takes hours for an officer to negotiate your life with a criminal. In extreme cases, they even risk their own lives to save another person. We have to appreciate that about someone who's willing to sacrifice his own life and safety for the benefit of others.

We also have situations where people get very selfish and have no control over their actions. A night out on the town with your friends may very well turn out to be the end of your existence on earth. It's late and you and your friends are driving back home and unbeknownst to you is that fool that was guzzling down shots of vodka because he felt he was man enough to handle it. His keys never left his pocket until he gets outside near his car. He's stumbling from the front exit all the way to his car, but that officer who is working detail at the club has been paying attention to him. He notices that the man is not in a condition to drive, so he summons his keys and places that man under arrest after he determines that the man is drunk. The "would be drunk driver" is now in police custody because an officer cared enough about the rest of us to keep us out of harm's way. That officer potentially saved your life and mine together because that man won't be on the road and you will make it home safe for one more night. Imagine that? There are actually officers out there like that, good officers.

Officers risk so much for the safety of the public they have to be appreciated and shown support, and I understand that. I'm grateful for my police department and I believe in being fair when a police officer is fair. Many of my friends are cops and I know what they go through on a daily basis because some of them talk about it. September eleventh was one of the worse days in New York City and New York's finest did a great job alongside New York's bravest. We'll forever be grateful to these guys who sacrificed their lives when many others were running away. It takes a tumultuous amount of heart and courage for someone to completely forgo his safety to save others.

Even in the comfort of our own home, when we fear that a possible intruder might be looming inside, we usually pick up the phone to call our devoted officers to come rescue us from potential danger. Our officers serve a great purpose and they're sometimes under appreciated for their efforts and it is okay to acknowledge that. However, at the same time we have the minority few who infiltrate the police force and have pulled a blanket of deception and corruption over the whole police department. These minority officers are basically polarizing a group of upstanding officers with their ill actions towards minority folks and society as a whole.

Now for the bad, just like the pimps and the gangs, there are officers whose purpose is to harass as many people as they possibly can because they are shielded by laws that allow them to get away with it. These are the officers who pose a threat to our well-being. Most of the time they are trigger-happy and are just waiting for a small reason to pull their gun out and start shooting. These officers accept no excuses whatsoever because they want to develop the reputation of hard asses. Most of the time that's enough reason for a red flag, but these officers are encouraged by the police department because the police department wants the toughest guys that can do the job.

Unfortunately, these hard ass officers are usually compensating for their fear. They try to instill fear in others while on the job in order to gain respect. Tough people don't have to prove that they tough to others.

It's something that is natural and a tough person hardly feels that his life is in danger all the time.

Police departments everywhere have also hired cops who are drug dealers, thieves and some that are involved in many other criminal activities. Often times, these cops aren't investigated properly before they're accepted into the police academy. A criminal can be a cop as long as he has never been caught doing criminal acts. As long as there is no record of criminal activities, a person can be a cop, it is that simple. The exam that is offered to potential officers by most cities can be passed if a person is smart enough to graduate from middle school. It is not that difficult.

There are many cops who take advantage of their badge and gun. They are on the street working for the drug dealers, the pimps and other organized crime, especially in New York City. It's very easy to buy cops in New York City because the salary that they are paid hardly brings them above the poverty line. It can be very enticing when a drug dealer offers a cop twenty to thirty thousand dollars to be a look-out. If that cop was already prone to illegal activities, then he's the perfect criminal cop.

The NYPD and other police departments would like to have the public believe that the process of becoming a cop is stringent, but I'd like to challenge that belief. I know and have met too many people who shouldn't be wearing a police uniform. The character flaws are easily noticeable, and most of the time, these people are one altercation away from killing someone for no reason. Since the law makes it okay for police officers to shoot at people when they deem it appropriate, the law should also make sure that these people are investigated properly before handing them a badge and a gun.

43

The Reality

The truth about all the murders that have taken place involving Black men around the country is that those shootings will continue to happen unless behaviors and attitudes are changed on both sides of the fence. The spin-doctoring on the part of police officers will continue as long they're allowed to justify their actions without proper investigations.

In most of the cases cited in this book, evidence of parallel investigation has been present. The cops are always going to look after their own first, regardless of right or wrong. People have to also understand that the reason that Black men are always at the tail of these incidents is because it's a systemic problem, not a racial one. Black cops have been trained to use their own prejudice towards their fellow black men. The fear for a black man always seems to be looming around in almost every aspect of life in this country.

Shooting victims are often embarrassed while in the hospital when they are handcuffed to the bed. This situation often instills fears in the nurses and the doctors who are supposed to care for them. Even though Trent Benefield committed no criminal act, he found himself handcuffed and shackled to the bed at the hospital after being shot by police for no reason. To make him appear as a criminal was the intent of the cops. It was the same with Guzman who barely survived with fifteen bullets in his body. The cops have no respect for Blacks and Latinos and they continue to show their disdain even in grave situations where they are the perpetrators of violence. Both victims were kept from their families while in the hospital as police continued to manipulate the whole incident and situation.

Even while being hooked up to a respirator the cops showed no respect to Guzman. He became a suspect in a case after his life was almost taken from him and no one seems to find anything wrong with the way these cops behaved. The behavior and the history of these bad cops reflect on every cop representing the NYPD. There will always be mistrust on the part of the black community because these cops don't respect the Black community. They feel as though that their laws are absolute and that there are no repercussions for their misbehavior.

The most dangerous aspect to this situation is that some of the black cops are part of this. While it's a well-known fact that most police departments use intimidation and threats against their own officers, but is it not a reason to say "enough is enough?" Threat of violence against suspects is a normal thing for the

NYPD and even when officers don't agree, they turn the other way because that's business as usual.

Police often will find the smallest reason to try to turn an acquaintance or a friend against a suspect. In the case of Sean Bell, police tried to turn Erskine Williams, Jr. aka BJ against his best friend, Trent Benefield-one of the shooting victims-after he was taken into custody for failure to pay a $25.00 ticket for loitering. While at the precinct, Williams was physically intimidated and one cop was even quoted to say "Look at the officer's hands. Look how big his hands are. Stop bullshitting us or else he's going to slam your fucking head against the wall." These cops try hard to be tough guys, but most of them should really be wearing skirts because they are nothing more than punks acting tough behind a badge and gun. Real tough guys don't pull out their weapon and shoot at innocent people without justification.

That's also another reality with the police department. They continue to hire these wimps who are too soft to fulfill the job requirement. They feel that tough the minute they're handed a badge and a gun after graduating from the police academy, knowing that they have an army of hundreds of thousands officers behind them to support them. I'm sure thorough background checks on most of the officers who have been involved in shootings of innocent victims would reveal the cowards that they really were before joining the police department. It takes a coward to pull a trigger on an unarmed man so many times, and the NYPD is full of cowards going around shooting innocent people because they are scared. These cops shouldn't work the streets if they're so afraid of them. Go back to your suburban haven and leave the City to those who have the heart to deal with the urbanites the right way.

The corrupted police union in New York City should also be investigated because they are the instigators in all of this. They are the ones trying to create men out of cowards and continue to jeopardize the lives of innocent people. They make these cops feel invincible and they fabricate stories and witnesses to exonerate them from murder charges and other misconduct behaviors.

There's also another reality and that's the reality that these cowardice cops will probably come after me as well. Unlike them, I'm no coward. I don't need a gun and a badge to walk around the hood feeling like a tough guy. I grew up in the hood most of my life and I've managed to survive with no problem. I don't fear other black men as society has been trying to brainwash me to do. I'm comfortable in my setting and when it's my time for the curtain call, I'll be ready. A soldier is always ready for war. A coward is always looking for a cowardice opportunity.

The threat of the NYPD coming around my family is very real, but I have no fear because I chose to take on this issue all on my own. A coward is going to be a coward and there's nothing that I can do about it. Some of the great men of the world like Malcolm X and Dr. Martin Luther King, Jr. have been killed by cowards, but they didn't die as cowards. A coward will die with fear in his heart. The NYPD needs to stop recruiting cowards to become police officers and perhaps only then that the shootings of innocent victims may stop.

Police officers are not the only cowards tormenting the hood, there are other types of cowards as well. Some of you may take offense to this, but I really don't give a damn. My list of enemies has been growing through each chapter, so why should I hold back now. It takes a big coward to feel that walking around his own neighborhood tormenting people with drugs and guns is okay. These cowards are the reasons why the other police cowards are shooting innocent victims. These two cowards seldom run into each other because they're both too scared of one another. Instead, they avoid each other at all cost, but torment people they have no business tormenting.

The drug dealers are nothing short of punks because the minute they notice a police cruiser with the real tough cops who want to help the community get peace of mind, they run like scared cats. "Here come popo! Just leave the shit and run!" some of them would say. Most of them are forced to become sprinters, long jump experts, pole vault jumpers, long distance runners and more at the site of police. These cowards are only tough with those who can't defend themselves in the hood when their only solace in life is usually found in a piece of rock due in part to their addiction. The good police officers have a hard time doing their jobs because of these cowards in the neighborhood. These cowards are too afraid to look for a legitimate job to live the lifestyle that they envy so much.

These cowards are also dumb and stupid because their cowardice asses usually end up where most cowards are too afraid to go, either dead or in jail. They may not get caught by the cowardice cops, but they will encounter many upstanding officers who want to honor the oath to protect and serve and when they come knocking, these cowards are usually taken away without a fight. You see, it's no secret that most cowards know who the tough guys are, but the problem is that they try to avoid the tough guys so much that they're blindsided most of the time by them. The cowards usually target innocent victims on which to prey. Drug dealers and dirty cops are both cut from the same cloth. The only difference between the two is that one carries a badge and a legal gun. Often times these cowards would link and form illegal relationships until they're discovered by the real tough guys in blue.

Make no mistake about it, I don't think that the NYPD is primarily made of cowards, but the percentage of cowards hired by the NYPD is getting higher and higher. Being a cop is almost like being a teacher. Some teachers would try to take advantage of their students for as long as they can until they are caught, and some teachers are talented and love their job so much that they only care about developing and creating the future doctors, engineers, teachers, and lawyers and so on. Most teachers are great for the classroom, but too many of them have fallen through the cracks and the victimized students usually end up paying the price. I believe that most cops are good for the community and some of them want to help rid the community of its bad elements, but not all cops come to the community with the same agenda. Some for them want to abuse their power and harass people for no reason and usually people have to pay the price with their lives when they encounter these dirty cops.

The reality is that we need good cops to help keep control and maintain order, but what we don't need is for bad cops to add to the chaos. We don't need trigger happy cops coming to the hood with their guns drawn like they're on the hunting field somewhere. These are the cops who have managed to manipulate a flawed system and once they become part of that system, they understand that they are supported and only total carelessness and utter disregard for their badge can rid them of their position. These cops' illegal actions usually go unnoticed for many years and by the time their true character is discovered a victim usually ends up shot many times by one of them. These are the tragedies that we need to take proactive steps to change, and the police departments need to make it clear to their officers that these ill behaviors won't be tolerated.

Another reality that I'm going to be faced with is the fact that many people, Black, White and other will probably label me an angry Black man, during or after reading this book. You're damn right I'm angry! If all that you've read didn't convince you that I have a right to be angry, then you missed the whole point of the book. How can we lessen the amount of angry Black men? Well for starters, they should be given an opportunity early in life. The school department has to do a better job educating these young men, thus lessen the risks of creating more criminals. There should be more funding for after-school programs as well as alternative training for those who don't necessarily find the classroom conducive. Because a person doesn't like the setting of a traditional classroom, it doesn't necessarily mean they can't learn a trade. Let's face it, not everyone is meant to go to college.

I'm not going to act as a problem-solver in this situation because this problem is way out of my league and too big for me to come up with all the solutions on my own. I hope this book opens the door for dialogue between police and the Black community as well as those elected officials who are supposed to look out for the best interest of their community. It's very easy for people to commit dishonorable acts when they're shown no appreciation for their efforts. A lot of police officers are not appreciated by the Black community because they have allowed a few bad cops to polarize their image. In order for someone to be courageous as an officer, that person has to fight for justice not just against civilian criminals, but also against criminal officers as well.

With everything said, I hope that all the dedicated officers who choose to read this book are able to remove themselves from the criticisms in this book because of their personal dedication to their job and the safety of the public. Some of us do appreciate your hard work in the community. But remember that if every time you see a fellow officer behaving inappropriately in your presence and you allow it to go on, you are just as guilty as that officer. It is almost like wiping your hand on the floor then washing it to find yourself going right back to the floor again.

Credits

Source: Louisiana Weekly Publishing Company
Author: Hazel Trice Edney, NNPA Washington Correspondent

Pub date: 2005

TWO POLICE SHOOTINGS SHOW UPSIDE-DOWN PRIORITIES OF DRUG WAR

Pubdate: Sun, 11 Feb 2001
Source: St. Louis Post-Dispatch (MO)
Copyright: 2001 St. Louis Post-Dispatch
Author: Bill McClellan

INNOCENT MAN DIES IN POLICE BLUNDER

Pubdate: Fri, 6 Oct 2000
Source: Tennessean, The (TN)
Copyright: 2000 The Tennessean
Author: Warren Duzak, Staff Writer

5 ON MIAMI SWAT TEAM FACING CHARGES

Pubdate: Thu, 15 Mar 2001
Source: San Jose Mercury News (CA)
Copyright: 2001 San Jose Mercury News
Contact: letters@sjmercury.com

LAWYERS CRITICIZE MCCULLOCH FOR CALLING SLAIN MEN "BUMS"

Pubdate: Sun, 07 Oct 2001
Source: St. Louis Post-Dispatch (MO)
Copyright: 2001 St. Louis Post-Dispatch
Author: William C Lhotka

OUTRAGE AT POLICE SHOOTING

Pubdate: Mon, 22 Apr 2002
Source: Newsday (NY)
Copyright: 2002 Newsday Inc.
Author: J. Jioni Palmer

TIP LED TO DEADLY RAID IN PREBLE

Pubdate: Sat, 05 Oct 2002
Source: Dayton Daily News (OH)
Copyright: 2002 Dayton Daily News
Author: Cathy Mong

MISTAKEN RAID DEATH IS RULED A HOMICIDE

Pubdate: Wed, 28 May 2003
Source: Detroit Free Press (MI)

Copyright: 2003 Detroit Free Press
Author: Unknown

Protest Of KY Suspect Shooting Gets Tense

Source: The Guardian Newspaper

Pubdate: January 9, 2004

Author: Unknown

Tape Reveals Terrifying Campaign In War On Drugs

Source: The Knoxville News-Sentinel

Pubdate: February 6, 2005

Author: Unknown

88-Year-Old Woman Is Latest Collateral Damage In Senseless Drug War

Pubdate: Mon, 04 Dec 2006
Source: Baltimore Sun (MD)
Copyright: 2006 The Baltimore Sun, a Times Mirror Newspaper.
Author: Cynthia Tucker
Note: Cynthia Tucker is editorial page editor for The Atlanta Journal-Constitution. Her column appears Mondays in The Sun.

Informant In Shooting Says He Never Bought Drugs At Home

Source: The Atlanta Journal of Constitution

Pubdate: November 27, 2006

50 Shots Fired, And The Experts Offer A Theory

Source: New York Times

Pubdate: November 27, 2006

Badges, Guns And Another Unarmed Victim

Source: New York Times

Author: Bob Herbert

Pubdate: November 30, 2006

In Seeking Clues To Police Shooting, A Search And Arrests

Source: New York Times

Pubdate: December 4, 2006

The Abner Louima case: three New York cops guilty in cover-up of torture

Source: World Socialist Website

Author: Bill Vann

Pubdate: March 9,2000

The Amadou Diallo case: The social and political roots of police violence

Source: World Socialist Website

Author: The editorial Board

Pubdate: February 28,2000

Special editorial on NYPD shootings by Daryl Khan

Article title: unknown.

Murder In Queens
by Walter Smith
New York Beacon
Originally posted 11/28/2006

To some in Paris, sinister past is back

Author: Howard Witt

Source: Chicago Tribune

PubDate: March 12, 2007

NEGLECTED SOULS
Richard Jeanty

Motherhood and the trials of loving too hard and not enough frame this story...The realism of these characters will bring tears to your spirit as you discover the hero in the villain you never saw coming...
Neglected Souls is a gritty, honest and heart stirring story of hope and personal triumph set in the ghettos of Boston.

Jimmy and Nina continue to feel a void in their lives because they haven't a clue about their genealogical make-up. Jimmy falls victims to a life threatening illness and only the right organ donor can save his life. Will the donor be the bridge to reconnect Jimmy and Nina to their biological family? Will Nina be the strength for her brother in his time of need? Will they ever find out what really happened to their mother? How will they handle the news about their mother? Will their grandparents Mr. and Mrs. Johnson have a change of heart about family situation? Find out as we explore the Johnson family further in the continuation of the struggle that Nina, Jimmy and the rest of the Johnson family have to face.

The Most Dangerous Gang in America: The NYPD

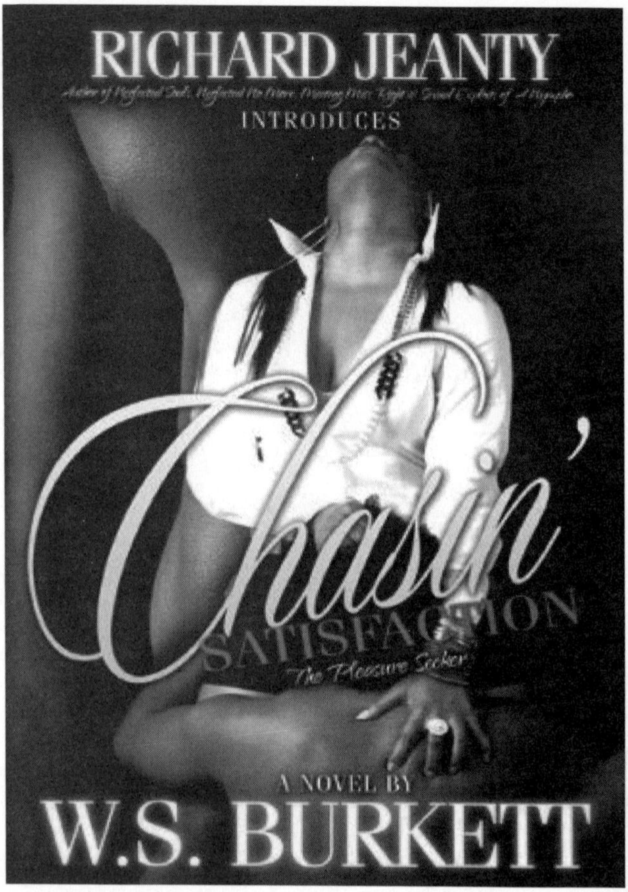

Betrayal, lust, lies, murder, deception, sex and tainted love frame this story... Julian Stevens lacks the ambition and freak ability that Miko looks for in a man, but she married him despite his flaws to spite an ex-boyfriend. When Miko least expects it, the old boyfriend shows up and ready to sweep her off her feet again. Suddenly the grass grows greener on the other side, but Miko is not an easily satisfied woman. She wants to have her cake and eat it too. While Miko's doing her own thing, Julian is determined to become everything Miko ever wanted in a man and more, but will he go to extreme lengths to prove he's worthy of Miko's love? Julian Stevens soon finds out that he's capable of being more than he could ever imagine as he embarks on a journey that will change his life forever.

Just when Darren thinks his relationship with Tina is flourishing, there is yet another hurdle on the road hindering their bliss. Tina saw a therapist for months to deal with her sexual addiction, but now Darren is wondering if she was ever treated completely. Darren has not been taking care of home and Tina's frustrated and agrees to a break-up with Darren. Will Darren lose Tina for good? Will Tina ever realize that Darren is the best man for her?

Coming September 2007

Ronald Murphy was a player all his life until he and his best friend, Myles, met the women of their dreams during a brief vacation in South Beach, Florida. Sexual Jeopardy is story of trust, betrayal, forgiveness, friendship and hope.

Coming February 2008

The Most Dangerous Gang in America: The NYPD

Malcolm is a wealthy virgin who decides to conceal his wealth From the world until he meets the right woman. His wealthy best friend, Dexter, hides his wealth from no one. Malcolm struggles to find love in an environment where vanity and materialism are rampant, while Dexter is getting more than enough of his share of women. Malcolm needs develop self-esteem and confidence to meet the right woman and Dexter's confidence is borderline arrogance.

Will bad boys like Dexter continue to take women for a ride?

Or will nice guys like Malcolm continue to finish last?

Tina develops an insatiable sexual appetite very early in life. She only loves her boyfriend, Darren, but he's too far away in college to satisfy her sexual needs.

Tina decides to get buck wild away in college
Will her sexual trysts jeopardize the lives of the men in her life?

Faith Jones, a woman in her mid-thirties, has given up on ever finding love again until she met her son's best friend, Darius. Faith Jones is walking a thin line of betrayal against her son for the love of Darius. Will Faith allow her emotions to outweigh her common sense?

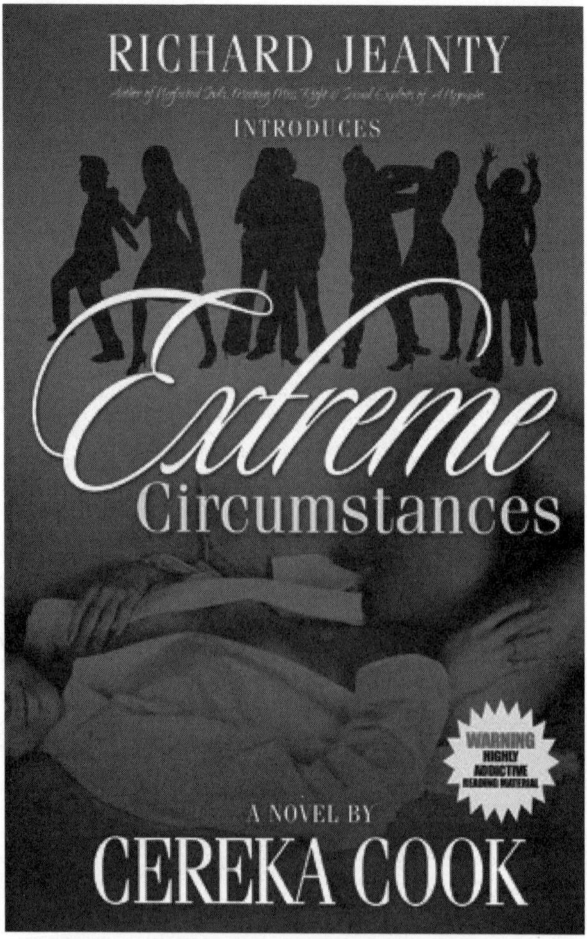

What happens when a devoted woman is betrayed? Come take a ride with Chanel as she takes her boyfriend, Donnell, to circumstances beyond belief after he betrays her trust with his endless infidelities. How long can Chanel's friend, Janai, use her looks to get what she wants from men before it catches up to her? Find out as Janai's gold-digging ways catch up with and she has to face the consequences of her extreme actions.

The Most Dangerous Gang in America: The NYPD

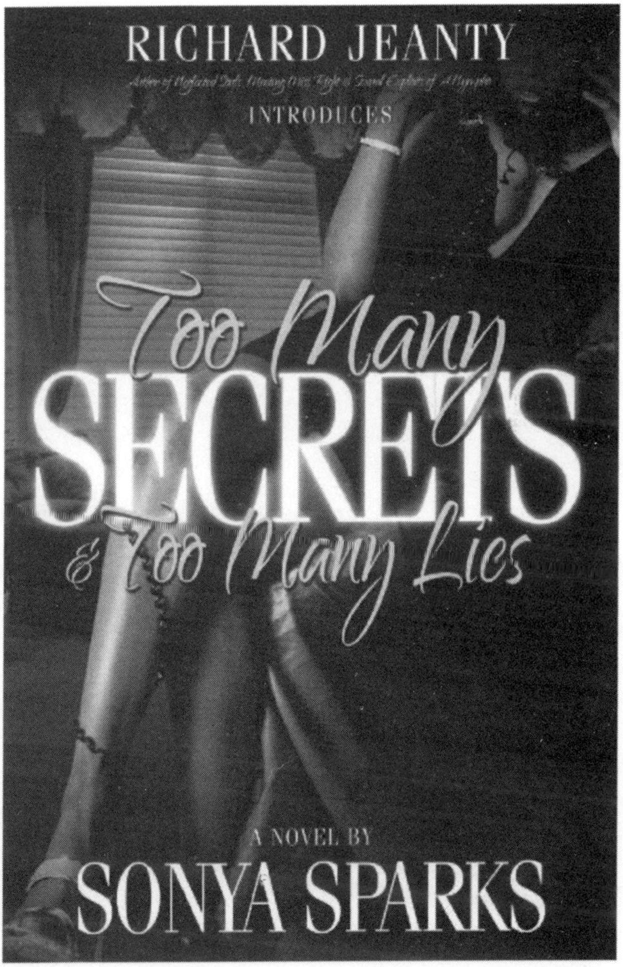

Coming summer 2007

PUBLICATIONS
BRINGING EXCITEMENT, FUN AND JOY TO READING

Available at bookstores everywhere
Use this coupon to order by mail

1. Neglected Souls (0976927713--$14.95)
2. Neglected No More (09769277--$14.95)
3. Sexual Exploits of Nympho (0976927721--$14.95)
4. Meeting Ms. Right(Whip Appeal) (0976927705-$14.95)
5. Me and Mrs. Jones (097692773X--$14.95)
6. Chasin' Satisfaction (0976927756--$14.95)
7. Extreme Circumstances (0976927764--$14.95)
8. The Most Dangerous Gang In America (0976927799-$15.00)
9. Sexual Exploits of a Nympho II (0976927772--$15.00) Coming Fall 2007
10. Sexual Jeopardy (0976927780--$14.95) Coming 02/08
11. Too Many Secrets, Too Many Lies $15.00 Summer 08

Name______________________________________
Address____________________________________
City________________State_____Zip Code_______

Please send the novels that I have circled above.

Shipping and Handling $1.99
Total Number of Books__________
Total Amount Due______________

This offer is subject to change without notice.
Send check or money order (no cash or CODs) to:

RJ Publications
290 Dune Street
Far Rockaway, NY 11691

For more information please call 718-471-2926, or visit
www.rjpublications.com

Please allow 2-3 weeks for delivery.

Order These Exciting Novels From

The Most Dangerous Gang in America: The NYPD

Order These Exciting Novels From

The Most Dangerous Gang in America: The NYPD

Order These Exciting Novels From

The Most Dangerous Gang in America: The NYPD